PEOPLE UNL

PEOPLE UNLIKE US
The India That Is Invisible

HarperCollins *Publishers* India

HarperCollins *Publishers* India Pvt Ltd
7/16 Ansari Road, Daryaganj, New Delhi 110 002

Copyright © HarperCollins *Publishers* India Pvt Ltd 2001

First Published 2001 by
HarperCollins *Publishers* India

ISBN 81-7223-427-9

Credits:
Javeed Shah for photographs on page nos. 1, 10, 14, 19, 29
Muzamil Jaleel for photograph on page no. 11
Outlook for photographs on page nos. 31, 36, 38, 42, 75, 78, 89, 91, 97, 125, 129, 133, 139
Sankarshan Thakur for photographs on page nos. 51, 58, 63, 71
K.M. Sharma for photographs on page nos. 101, 104, 108, 116, 122
Bandeep Singh for photograph on page no. 149
Susan Bullough for photographs on page nos. 159, 168, 171, 195, 210

Typeset in Elegant Garamond by
Nikita Overseas Pvt Ltd
19A, Ansari Road
New Delhi 110 002

Printed in India by
Rekha Printer Pvt Ltd
A-102/1 Okhla Industrial Area
New Delhi 110 020

All rights reserved. No part of this publication may be reproduced, stored in a retrieval system, or transmitted, in any form or by any means, electronic, mechanical, photocopying, recording or otherwise, without the prior permission of the publishers.

Contents

From the Publisher		*vii*
Muzamil Jaleel	Invisible Grief	1
Sagarika Ghose	The Economics of Sati	31
Sankarshan Thakur	Still There	51
Siddhartha Deb	Fragments From a Folder	75
Ajit Kumar Jha	War in a Time Warp	101
Meenal Baghel	Lull After the Storm	125
Vijay Jung Thapa	Maid in India	149
Randhir Khare	'Do Rats Have Rights ?'	159
Notes on Contributors		213

From the Publisher

People Unlike Us — The India That Is Invisible is the third in the Contemporary Essays series by HarperCollins India, the first two being *Guns and Yellow Roses — Essays on the Kargil War* and *On the Abyss — Pakistan After the Coup*.

These experiments in interpretative journalism have been critically acclaimed, and have proved to be a valuable complement to the media and public discourse on the subjects of Kargil and Pakistan. In fact, the *raison d'etre* of the Contemporary Essays series, as we explained in the Pakistan book, is to take an in-depth look at subjects of recent importance — from major news events to social trends and popular culture — in an attempt to rise above and go beyond the media's handling of these issues. The idea is to look at these issues by taking a couple of steps back. Hoping that the farther back you step, the better you can look at the big picture.

With this in mind, when we were thinking of doing a book on what the new millennium means for India, we thought it appropriate to look for stories that the media was not doing, though these were staring it in the face. We decided to take a look at the India we have no time or patience for — the people we choose not to see, the places that are falling off the map, and the attitudes and mind-sets that remain unchanged.

To an extent it is understandable why this India gets marginalised in the media. The mainstream media, with some very visible exceptions (the writers in this anthology are a testament to this) has of late been changing its focus — perhaps because of justifiable economic reasons — from the world outside to the world of its readers, to the world of People Like Us. In this English-speaking middle class world, events like Kargil and the dotcom phenomenon occupy much more mindspace, and thus there aren't enough compelling reasons for newspapers to invest in stories from the margins.

Second, there is no real pressure, either from within the media or from outside (from the readers), for a greater attempt at understanding these issues. The media's focus is shifting to what in newsrooms is called the "aspirational story": stories that the reader somehow aspires to be a part of — society gatherings, fashion shows, celebrity gossip.

At a deeper level, this attitude also explains the obvious difference in the media's coverage of two recent natural calamities — the supercyclone in Orissa and the earthquake in Gujarat. The victims of the earthquake were visibly from the urban middle class, in a state that ranks No. 1 in the country in terms of attracting foreign investment, and which has a huge diaspora of resourceful nonresident Indians. The media therefore went to town in its coverage of the earthquake, with detailed stories about the nexus between unscrupulous builders and corrupt politicians. The cyclone in Orissa, in contrast, did not attract this kind of coverage — it affected people who had fallen off the map even before the cyclone hit them. These were people who did not read English newspapers.

Once we had decided to focus on stories that don't get done, we knew that these had to be done by journalists with a certain sensitivity. We found in our previous two books that there are journalists out there capable of taking a step back

FROM THE PUBLISHER

and approaching and writing stories differently, and who welcome a platform like this that allows them to escape their normal work, space and deadline pressures. One common strain in the essays, therefore, is a deliberate attempt by the writers to put faces to these stories, to bring a sense of the past to these stories as well as a sense of empathy, so that the stories don't remain just names on Page One but get transformed into stories of real lives, real people.

It was an ambitious project, and there are many things this book does not have — for instance, there is nothing here on child labour, or what labour is going through in this age of economic reforms or the mass exodus from the villages to the cities — but we see this not as a definitive book, but as a first step towards providing a forum for stories that get ignored by the media. We hope to do more such books in the future.

Wherever the writers went — in Kashmir and the Northeast, in the villages of Bihar and Uttar Pradesh, in the tribal interiors of Madhya Pradesh and Maharashtra, in cyclone-ravaged Orissa — they found a sense of alienation among these "invisible" Indians. There was also a sense of rage, often silent, and grief, often invisible, at being left behind, ignored, unheard...a rage and grief that was left unarticulated at times and which our writers have given an expression to.

Thus writer Muzamil Jaleel went into two remote villages in north Kashmir and discovered a tiny tragic world — very early in the militant movement, the army had massacred people in one village, while the militants took their toll in the other. The villagers are still haunted by the memories, still grieving, still demanding justice...alienated from all, forgotten by everyone.

FROM THE PUBLISHER

Siddhartha Deb, who spent his childhood in Shillong, felt the same kind of frustration when writing about the neglect and alienation of the North-east: Secession for these states, he says, "is simply an act of ratification, a cofirmation of their alien status, an attempt on their part to make the contract bilateral so that they may be as free of mainland India as India is free of them."

There is also the plain old desperation of living on the edge: When Sagarika Ghose went to investigate an incident of sati in Satpurva village in Uttar Pradesh, instead of finding villagers with obscurantist mind-sets still living in the Dark Ages, she encountered people so economically backward, they just wanted to get some money for the village out of the sati incident — they didn't care whether it was a sati or suicide!

There is also fatalism here combined with a sense of loss — and proof that in some respects, such as on the issue of caste, India hasn't changed at all. Sankarshan Thakur revisited Mehrana village in Uttar Pradesh ten years after he first went there to cover the public hanging of a young couple — a Yadav boy and a Jat girl — for eloping. The hanging had been ordered by a Jat-dominated panchayat to teach the Chamars in the village a lesson: "Never touch our women again." Ten years on, in the new millennium, the village has a Chamar sarpanch, but only in name, and only because of the reservation system — nothing has actually changed in the village, and the Jats continue to dominate like they always have. Could there be a repeat of the hangings in Mehrana? "Our boys will never commit such a mistake again," says the sarpanch.

There are other such stories of an India caught in a time

FROM THE PUBLISHER

warp. Ajit Kumar Jha travelled through Bihar's Jehanabad district, where landless labourers have dared to challenge the might of the landlords, leading to an economic blockade, a breakdown in social relations, and gang-based killings by both sides. The labourers want an increase in wages but the landlords, still nursing a feudal streak, would have none of it, and the standoff has lasted for over a decade. Today, the landlords think of every Dalit in the village as a Naxalite while for the backwards, every Bhumihar is a potential member of the Ranvir Sena, the private army of the landlords. Both sides keep night-long vigils to guard against each other.

In Orissa, where people didn't have much to begin with, the supercyclone washed away lives, but its aftermath snuffed out dignity. While the victims were shell-shocked, the administration was paralysed. Meenal Baghel, who travelled through the region, reports that a year and a half after the calamity, the state is no better prepared to deal with a cyclone, and many affected people are still waiting for the state to provide them with a semblance of basic amenities.

Sometimes people lose more than their dignity — their identity itself. Deep in the interiors of Madhya Pradesh, in Jhabua district, and in the foothills of the Western Ghats in Maharashtra, Randhir Khare spent time empathising with the Bhils and the Katkaris — tribals who have lost their way of life and are now in limbo. He makes an impassioned plea for us to first start understanding them before thrusting any kind of development plans on them.

And then there is the invisible Indian inside our own homes — the servants who slog relentlessly for us for a pittance. We see them but yet we don't — we see them only as slaves.

FROM THE PUBLISHER

Vijay Jung Thapa tells the story of a maid from Darjeeling who works sixteen hours a day for Rs 2,000 a month.

The key to economic reforms is transparency, competition, accountability and most important of all, a level playing field. What these stories tell us is that the playing fields are not, and can never be, level. It is the story of an India where systems of patronage, caste domination, and of little or no accountability are still in place. It's the story of an India that either we don't see or don't want to see.

INVISIBLE GRIEF

■ MUZAMIL JALEEL

> The story of two remote villages along the Line of Control in Kashmir. The army massacred people in one, the militants in the other. Today, the villagers grieve alone, silently… forgotten by everyone, and alienated from all.

INVISIBLE GRIEF

I was born here. I grew up in these apple orchards, dreamed on the banks of these freshwater streams. I went to school here, sitting on straw mats and memorising tables by heart. After school my mates and I would rush halfway home, tearing off our uniforms and diving into the cold water. Then we would quickly dry our hair, so our parents would not find out what we had done. Sometimes, when we felt especially daring, we would skip an entire day of school to play cricket.

I was here, too, when the first bomb was exploded in 1988. I remember my father describing the blast as an opposition party plot to dislodge Farooq Abdullah's government. I was seventeen. Then, that September, the killing in Srinagar of Ajaz Dar, one of the first Kashmiri youths to become a militant leader, changed everything. Bomb blasts and shootouts became frequent. As 1989 came, the situation worsened. For days the morning papers splashed photos of five fugitives — Ishfaq Majeed, Javeed Mir, Yasin Malik, Hameed Sheikh and Shabir Shah — who were believed to be behind the rising unrest and violence. The government offered a huge reward to anybody who gave information about them, but nobody came forward. This was not a simple political game any more. It was war.

I had just completed Class XII then and was enrolled in college — a perfect potential recruit. Many of my close friends and classmates had begun to join the militant movement. One day, half of our class in a Sopore college was missing. They never returned to class again, but nobody even looked for them, because it was understood. I too wanted to join, not knowing why or what it would lead to. Perhaps the rebel image was subconsciously attracting all of us. I acquired the standard militant's gear: I bought Duckback rubber shoes, prepared a polythene jacket and trousers to wear over my warm clothes, and found some woollen cloth to wrap around my calves as protection from frostbite. I stole five hundred rupees from my mother's purse to pay the guide.

But I failed. Thrice we returned from the border. Each time something happened that forced our guide to take us back. The third time, twenty-three of us had started our journey on foot from Malangam, north of Bandipore, only to be abandoned inside a dense jungle. It was night and the group scattered after hearing gunshots nearby, sensing the presence of security forces. In the morning, when we gathered again, the guide was missing. Most of the others decided to try their luck and continue on their own, but a few of us turned back. We had nothing to eat but leaves for three days. We followed the flights of crows, hoping to reach a human settlement. We were lucky. We reached home and survived.

As the days and months passed, and the routes the militants took to cross the border became known to security forces, the bodies started arriving. Lines of young men would disappear on a ridge as they tried to cross over or return home. The stadiums where we had played cricket and soccer, the beautiful green parks where we had gone on school excursions as small kids in white and grey uniforms, were turned into martyrs' graveyards. One after another, those who used to play there were buried there with huge marble epitaphs detailing their sacrifice. Many had not even fired a single bullet from their Kalashnikovs.

When I started writing about the war in 1992, I felt I was part of this tragic story from the beginning. I knew the mujahids, the *mukhbirs* (informers), those who surrendered and those who did not, those who faced death because they had a dream and those who were sacrificed by mere chance, neither knowing nor understanding the issues at stake, those who believed they were fighting a holy war and those who joined for unholy reasons.

After eight years of reporting death and suffering, I felt I knew every bit of the trauma of Kashmir. I had seen a thousand widows wailing over their sons' graves, mothers of militants and mothers of policemen alike. I had seen villages burnt to the ground by security forces, bodies blown to bloody bits by militant bombs, bodies blackened by torture in interrogation centres. I had met families with no children left, no food left, no hope left. I thought I had reported the whole truth about Kashmir.

Then, one day, I travelled to a remote corner of north Kashmir, along the Line of Control. I took my time, and wandered into two small villages, speaking to everyone I met, and asking them to tell me their stories. What I discovered was a tiny world of silent tragedy and invisible suffering — suffering that no headlines had reported, no government officials had compensated, and that virtually no one knew about beyond the village boundaries.

While many other villages in Kashmir had been struck by violence, few had experienced such extensive tragedy so early in the uprising, and few had borne their grief in such isolation. Officials had visited the two villages, and promises had been made and forgotten. But with time, as the real suffering sank in and became part of the lore and emotions and fabric of these villages, there was no one to console them.

In both cases, anonymous people had died as cannon fodder, not as heroes to either side of the cause.

As the incidents receded into the past, the villages, isolated and invisible, grieved alone. The rest of Kashmir, caught up in a whirlpool of violence, seemed to have no time or energy to spare for them. To the India beyond, the villages had never existed even before the massacres. Afterward, they existed only as abstract symbols to be politically exploited by India — in one case as evidence of Pakistan-sponsored terrorism, and in the other as an unavoidable consequence of militancy. Pakistan, in turn, kept silent on the first massacre and capitalised on the second as proof of atrocities by the Indian security forces.

But for the survivors in these remote villages, who knew little about the politics being played over their dead, the enormity of what had happened haunted their lives every day. Even now, virtually every house is a portrait of loss and gloom; nearly every family hides a tragedy.

There is a girl who wanders the graveyard where her two brothers are buried, muttering to herself. There is another who was raped by armymen, and the family and the village kept it a secret. There is a man wracked by guilt because, in trying to be loyal to India, he condemned his neighbours and relatives to death. There is a woman who was forced to marry a boy she had once cradled in her arms, after her own husband was killed. There is a mother who still curses herself for keeping her son home for an extra day of holiday — it proved to be his last. There was a boy who was killed by militants just seven days after his wedding, with henna still on his palms. There is a widow who used to boil water in an empty pot to give her children false hope of dinner. There is another who has to beg to feed her children, who has no one to follow her slain husband's case and no money to bribe the clerks.

The stories of these two forgotten villages, both situated in the frontier district of Kupwara, are different from each other. In Warsun, the people had resisted the tide of militancy and were punished by the militants for garlanding a Union minister. And yet the authorities did not believe that a village so close to the Line of Control could be entirely innocent, so they too punished the people for what they assumed was a self-protective lie.

A man who lost twenty-two of his relatives to militant attacks had his own son killed in the custody of the security forces. Another man who launched the first ever indigenous counter-insurgent group to help the army, and escaped death six times, saw his cousin's head chopped off by militants. He still bears a scar from a militant attack on his shoulder, a badge of his Indianness, and yet even that was not enough to keep a security force officer from plotting to take his life. Today, he lives in fear from both sides.

The other hamlet, Pazipora, a dozen miles from Warsun, was the site of one of the first, and biggest, massacres by the army in August 1990. So bloody and massive was the attack that the armymen ran out of cartridges. Twenty-four people died there that day as bullets rained from all sides. In the evening, there was an announcement on the radio. General Zaki, the then security advisor to the governor, claimed that the army had killed twelve militants. Later, after the bodies were identified, the government's story too changed: Now it was twelve young militants and twelve old villagers dead.

It took this village over three-and-a-half years and thousands of rupees to prove that their dead were innocent civilians, killed by the army in retaliation for a militant attack on their convoy on the main road outside the village. All through that period, their cries of protest were not heard, their demand for justice ignored. And till today, the most awful truth of the Pazipora massacre has never been told: the rape of three unmarried girls after the armymen segregated the men and women of the village. The villagers kept it a secret to avoid problems in finding matches for these girls. But in silence, the families still mourn for their lost honour.

One survivor of the Pazipora massacre has never spoken about it at all. Each day, in the village graveyard, a young woman walks in circles around two of the graves, murmuring to herself. She had never been mentally well as a child, and the shock of her brothers' violent deaths drove her deeper into madness, locking away the tragedy inside her. In this invisible corner of India, her pain is the most invisible of all.

■

*Yes, I remember it,
the day I'll die, I broadcast the crimson,*

*so long ago of that sky, its spread air,
its rushing dyes, and a piece of earth*

*bleeding, apart from the shore, as we went
on the day I'll die, past the guards, and he,*

*keeper of the world's last saffron, rowed me
on an island the size of a grave. On*

INVISIBLE GRIEF

two yards he rowed me into the sunset,
past all pain. On everyone's lips was news

of my death but only that beloved couplet,
broken, on his:

"If there is a paradise on earth,
It is this, it is this, it is this."

— From *The Country Without a Post Office,*
by Agha Shahid Ali

Warsun lies at the end of a steep, winding road, deep in a mountain range known for its hidden treasure of marble and a variety of medicinal herbs. It is a Gujjar village of some four hundred inhabitants, who live in small houses of mud walls and thatched roofs, scattered across small hillocks.

Only a few miles north lies the Line of Control. The elders dare not venture into the jungles because it is too dangerous — either militant territory, or an area controlled by the army. Beyond the hilltops, the villagers say, nobody can guarantee your life because bullets fly without warning from any direction. In a way, death seems to stalk these mountains.

The village has a school, but the majority of children cannot afford to study. Their job is to graze small herds of cows and goats. Forty-nine of them were orphaned in these ten years of mayhem. Smeared with dirt, they walk through corn fields on narrow footpaths, but there is no sound of their laughter or games. In fact, there is almost no sound at all. The village seems completely deserted.

Forty-nine children were orphaned in Warsun in ten years of mayhem. Instead of studying, they now graze goats.

Before the emergence of militancy, people remember, the hills used to echo with the sound of flutes played by the young shepherds. Now there are hardly any young men left. The few who remain wield guns and belong to a small counter-insurgency group, the Muslim Liberation Army of Choudhary Jalaluddin. They are the only wealthy people in the village, and their houses are more solidly built than the rest.

Many of the villagers died simply because they were related to the Choudharys and stood by them, even though they had no politics of their own. In some cases their widows were forced to marry their brothers, even those who already had

INVISIBLE GRIEF

wives, so that the family fortunes would not be divided. Widows were even forced to beg in the surrounding villages to feed their children. Today, the village is still fighting to survive, and its people have little time to think about the past. But every household in Warsun has a story to offer — a sordid saga of pain and loss.

Choudhary Jalaluddin is a tall, bearded man in his early forties — he is also the villager with the heaviest cross to bear. For most of his life, he was a shepherd and had

In happier times: The target of militants as well as the security forces, Jalaluddin (extreme right) has lost twenty-three of his family and friends. "No one here is Indian at heart, nor will anybody save you for being Indian."

nothing to do with politics. But after the emergence of militancy in 1990, his life became a tortuous roller coaster of shifting political demands and loyalties, physical hardships and betrayals, and survival amid death — all leading him to the bitter conclusion that no cause was sacred and no friend was permanent.

The first stage in his tumultuous path began when he crossed over to become a militant. "I never wanted to cross over to Pakistan. I never wanted to become a militant," he recalls. "There was a man, Farooq Molvi, who was very powerful for he was close to both (Indian and Pakistani) intelligence agencies. As a double agent, he was sending young men across for training. He had political scores to settle with my elder brother Choudhary Salamuddin and my cousin Alif Din, and I became his easy prey." Molvi had influence among militant ranks, and had a hit-order issued in his name. "I got to know and literally went underground to avoid certain death," he recalls. "This is when the police also started looking for me, suspecting me to be an activist of the Jammu and Kashmir Liberation Front (JKLF)."

On the run, Jalaluddin was caught between the devil and the deep sea. His cattle and sheep got scattered because there was nobody to take care of them. The police raided his house and even took away the fodder he had stored for the winter months. "I had no money to buy food or clothes for my family," he remembers. "I started selling off the cattle, partly for survival and partly because I could not afford their fodder." Then Master Afzal, a member of the JKLF from the neighbouring Trehgam village, was released from jail. Afzal promised to take Jalaluddin across the border and guaranteed his safety there. "I talked to my elder brother about it, but he was dead against my joining militancy. He was a Congressy (activist of the Congress party) and an Indian to the core of his heart."

Jalaluddin decided to go anyway. He had formed a group of two hundred and fifty men and twelve guides, and they were planning to cross via Aawra village. "All the guides were from Aawra and knew the entire border like the lines on their hands," he said. "Even my nephew Ali Mohammad, who ran a hotel in Kupwara, was there. Those days hundreds of young men would cross from almost everywhere in this belt. It was safe and easy. After we crossed over, I saw Farooq Molvi at Athmuqam. He had been waiting for me and tried to get me off the bus and kidnap me, but my companions resisted."

The group remained in Muzzafarabad for seven months. At first, no one in the training camp trusted them, thinking them to be Indian agents. "Nobody believed us. Nobody helped us," he said. "My nephew and I had to eat raw rice with water and molasses. We saw so much suffering that even today we cry when we remember those days. Finally, when the people running the camps decided we were not Indian agents, they gave us shelter." To earn some money, Jalaluddin and his friends guided groups of newly trained militants to the border posts, to infiltrate into the valley. "We used the money to buy oil and salt and keep ourselves going. As time passed, trust started developing and the next few months went well."

Then Jalaluddin heard that his cousin, Alif Din, had been killed by unidentified gunmen back home. He was a sarpanch and had been killed by militants, who were avenging some old slight. Jalaluddin was allowed to return for a week.

Salamuddin's (extreme right) son was tortured to death by the security forces, and he himself nearly met the same fate.

"I reached the village and saw my brother, Choudhary Salamuddin, half dead from torture — this time by the security forces," he recalled. "His son, Abdullah, had also been tortured to death by the Central Reserve Police Force. The situation was confusing, and I felt everyone was against me and my family. I heard that a group of fifty militants led by Farooq Molvi's brother had raided my house. I tried to convince them to stop, arguing that this group clash would take us nowhere. But they would not listen. I felt bitter. I had my own militant group, the Muslim Liberation Army, and I decided to take them on."

It was 1991. The war between the two groups went on for six months. Jalaluddin had only thirteen gunmen, but they managed to keep a group of three hundred and fifty militants at bay. "At times I was frightened, but I never allowed it to show," he says. "This was my village, my area, how could I allow anybody to win here? It was a battlefield of my choice." But then his enemies played a trick, and one of his men, Fareed Shah, turned out to be a mole. "One day he guided the troops of 7 Assam Rifles to my hideout. The only escape was to go up to the jungle, but there were seventy militants of that rival group up on every ridge, waiting to shoot me," Jalaluddin recounts. "Down below was the army. What could I do? I decided my only choice was to surrender."

It was a big catch. The first time that a commander-in-chief of a militant group had been nabbed. "They took me to the GOC. I had already decided to go against the militants," he says. "I wanted to teach them a lesson. I gave a plan to the army as to how to deal with the militants. They trusted me and I helped them. I opened the way for others to surrender, and created an opening for politics. I created the road, which nobody knew then, and now even much bigger convoys than mine are travelling on it."

Jalaluddin claims to have been instrumental in creating a counter-militancy movement, the first insider to challenge the might of the pro-Pakistan militants. "My fight started bearing fruit when militants like Kuka Parrey, Rasheed Khan and Azad Nabi followed suit to help the authorities control the militancy," he says. In 1992, he boasts, he and his associates were the first to hold a pro-India political rally in the area. "We garlanded the then Union internal security minister Rajesh

Pilot in Warsun and organised a huge gathering to listen to his speech right here. Then we conducted several such rallies in other villages in Kupwara. It was an unbelievable thing. We did it, but we paid a price. Those of our cousins who garlanded Pilot sahib were kidnapped and killed within a few days."

But it was not only militants who were after his blood. "In 1996, an officer of the (army) Liaison Unit conspired to kill me. I later got to know that he was given a car as a gift by my old enemies to eliminate me, but God saved me and I am alive. Even a senior police officer of the district was after my life for reasons not known to me till today. My covering candidate in the elections was killed by a surrendered militant. He was given a booty of three lakh rupees to eliminate the man. Now I have joined the ruling National Conference — but only to keep myself alive. At least now I am close to the corridors of power, and I feel a bit secure, though the fear still hangs over my head like a sword."

Through the years of war, Jalaluddin lost twenty-three of his cousins, relatives and friends. "At the end of the day, I am a depressed man," he says. "I feel responsible for the bloodshed and tragedy of my entire village. I am not able to face the widows of my brothers, who were killed for being with me." As long as the army was in the village, they would send foodgrains for these families. But as the militants mounted pressure in other areas, the army camp here was moved. "Now there are days when there is nothing to cook and eat," Jalaluddin says. "What can I do? I still have nothing to offer them except pain and suffering. I can't afford the cost of their two meals a day. I wish the militants or the police had managed to kill me in the beginning. Then, children of only one household would have been orphaned, not those of the entire village."

Depressed by his solitary burden, Jalaluddin says he at times envies those who died for Pakistan. "At least they have somebody to shed tears for them. There are people who visit their families and enquire about their wellbeing. But we have neither this world nor the world hereafter," he complains. "Everyone feels the blood that was shed here for India has gone to waste. After eight years of experience with the government, I have come to the conclusion that beneath every chair lies a *chor*. I now strongly feel the best way to live is in the jungles. You fire a few bullets and kill a few enemies, or get a few bullets and die. The story ends there and then. In political life, nothing is clean. No one here is Indian at heart, nor will anybody save you for being Indian. It is altogether a different game, with no permanent rules, no permanent enemies, no permanent friends."

■

Weeping, wailing, lamentation,
Piercing through the silent night,
Cries of children and their mothers,
The moon and stars sorrow-soaked,
The night crowned with weeping stars...
The night has nothing to show but dark.

— Makhdoom Mahiuddin

For the women of Warsun, the war was not a confusing cauldron of rapidly shifting political events, but the legacy of a single, violent incident that forever shattered their lives. There are more than a dozen widows in this village whose husbands died in the violence. They were the hardest hit of all victims, yet they never knew why such tragedies struck them. They were all illiterate. They never understood the nuances of Indo-Pak hostility, the politics of militancy and counter-insurgency. They had no say in the lives of their husbands and little control over their own lives after being widowed. Even when asked to recount their personal tragedies, they defer to male relatives to speak for them. They are the most invisible victims of all.

Arsha does not remember her age. She looks frail and careworn. An elderly neighbour believes she is about forty. She lost her husband, Mohammad Din, in 1992 in a militant attack. He was neither a militant nor a counter-insurgent. He was a simple farmer who had gone to fetch a missing calf from the meadow, never to return alive. He was hit by bullets and was carried home but died on the way. Mohammad Din, in fact, was killed merely for being the first cousin of Choudhary Jalaluddin, and more precisely for accompanying Jalaluddin on that fatal day.

"He was outside his house, preparing to start for the meadow to look for his calf, when I saw him," recalls Jalaluddin, speaking on Arsha's behalf as she sits silently across the room, weeping. "I had to visit the nearby army brigade headquarters and asked Mohammad Din to come along." They both left for the jungles where, on the way, they were attacked by the militants. "I received a bullet in my shoulder but ducked down on the ground. He too was lying flat but he thought I had been killed and shouted for me. This is when the militants shot at him," he says.

After she lost her husband in a militant attack, Arsha was married off to his nephew, a boy she had raised as her own.

Arsha lives in a small two-room house which she shares with her three children, her cow and a few sheep. There are a few aluminium utensils, two mattresses and some old blankets for bedding. For the first four years after her husband's death, she fought the hardships of life single-handedly, feeding her children by begging and working as a daily wage labourer in neighbouring villages. Finally the village elders met and decided she needed to remarry. Choudhary Jalaluddin admits he forced her to marry her late husband's nephew, even though he was half her age and had even been cradled by her in her arms.

Arsha had no option. She either had to leave her children behind with no one to take care of them and go back to her parents' home, or accept the trauma of marrying a boy she had raised like her son. Even her parents were not ready to take her in, so she had to accept the harsh verdict of the elders. Arsha does not speak easily about her trauma, but after repeated queries she bursts into a litany of grief and sorrow.

"I don't know what is the reason for this bloodshed. I remember my husband's last few moments. It seemed as if the entire world was crying. He was trying to tell me something, but I couldn't hear. He asked for water, and he asked for his son Fareed. Then his eyes closed. Later, they forced me to marry my *poot*, a boy I had raised like my own. But still nothing has changed."

"I have three children — two daughters, Shakeela and Zaitoon, and a son, Fareed. They have nothing to eat or wear. Many a time I boiled water on the mud oven to keep the hope for food alive when they were starving. They waited and waited for dinner as I kept telling them to wait just a few more minutes, until they fell asleep on empty stomachs. I have begged for months to get food to keep them alive. Nobody ever came to ask me whether I needed anything. The army camp nearby sent rations for a few months after my husband's killing, but later nobody cared. When the wound is fresh everybody comes to console you, but as time passes it becomes an old story."

INVISIBLE GRIEF

There is another widow in the village named Arsha. The death of her husband, Taj Din, in 1993 was even more tragic, but she too does not speak of it publicly. She has been silenced by remarriage to her late husband's brother, who already had a wife and children. Though marrying a brother-in-law after a husband's death is an old custom in Kashmiri villages, it has been used more frequently during militancy to avoid any split in family fortunes, especially when there is hope for ex gratia relief of one lakh rupees or a government job for close relatives of the person killed in violence. Arsha's new husband, Alif Din, talks on her behalf.

"Taj Din had garlanded Pilot sahib at the rally. After a few days his six-year-old daughter, Jameela, fell ill. She had pneumonia and needed immediate medical care. Taj Din rushed her to a doctor in Trehgam. He got a prescription and was about to enter a medical store when a young man called him. He paid no heed, but then a few more men gathered and took him away forcibly. He had to abandon his ailing daughter.

"They took him (Taj Din) to the government school building in Heeri village and interrogated him. Then they took him to Doripora and tortured him. They took out the thin iron rod from a Kalashnikov (a ramrod, used to clean the barrel). They put this rod in the fire and waited till it was red hot. They then pierced it through his chest. He asked for water but they put a lump of earth in his mouth instead. At Avera culvert, they pumped four bullets into his chest. He died on the spot.

"When Taj Din was kidnapped, another of our brothers, who also happened to be in the market, saw Jameela crying near the chemist's shop and carried her back home but without any medicine. The entire family was so traumatised that they literally forgot about the girl and her illness. She died the next day because she had received no medical care. And just as we were about to take her coffin to the graveyard, her father's body arrived. They were buried side by side."

■

> "Don't tell my father I have died," he says,
> and I follow him through blood on the road
> and hundreds of pairs of shoes the mourners
> left behind, as they ran from the funeral,
> victims of the firing. From windows we hear
> grieving mothers, and snow begins to fall
> on us, like ash. Black on edges of flames,
> it cannot extinguish the neighbourhoods,
> the homes set ablaze by midnight soldiers.
> Kashmir is burning.
>
> — From *The Country Without a Post Office*,
> by Agha Shahid Ali

Barely a dozen miles from Warsun, on the other side of Kupwara, lies Pazipora village. Deep in the apple orchards and paddy fields of this frontier district, it looks like any other Kashmiri village. Unlike Warsun, though, it is situated down a slope. In fact, the lane leading to it from the main road dips sharply until it reaches a secluded hollow. This accident of geography has had much to do with Pazipora's misfortune.

INVISIBLE GRIEF

On one fateful day in 1990, soldiers firing downward caught its people with no place to hide from the raining bullets.

Pazipora is the site of one of Kashmir's many forgotten massacres, the scars of which are still to heal. Even after a gap of ten years, the villagers remember it as if it had happened yesterday. The events of 10 August 1990 have become part of village folklore. It is a history lesson that every mother gives her child as compulsory information.

The village lost twenty-four of its sons that day. Not a single one was a militant. Their misfortune was that militants had ambushed an army convoy returning from a crackdown operation in a nearby village, perhaps killing a few soldiers in the process. In response, the panic-stricken army jawans let loose a reign of terror.

Today, Pazipora is an open wound. Geographically, it is still a part of India, but emotionally it is poles apart. What festers is not only the memory of the massacre itself, but of the official apathy to the suffering it caused. In many other villages of Kashmir, force was used to combat militancy. But here, soldiers went berserk and punished civilians for a crime they never committed. The government eventually acknowledged the atrocity, and each victim's family received a routine one lakh rupees ex gratia relief. But they never got back their sense of belonging or faith. They had believed the perpetrators would be punished, but they never were. Thus the wounds could never be fully healed, the gulf never bridged. After this, Pazipora would never really belong to India.

"No one among those killed that day had guns in their hands, no relative of the dead became a militant even after that tragedy. Why did the government not take any action against the culprits?" an old man asks. "If we are part of India, why are our lives so cheap? Where is the justice? Even if they have taken action against their officers, it means nothing to us until we see it with our own eyes. Why can't we demand gallows for them, they who spilled the blood of two dozen men in a single day?"

In all of Pazipora, Bhat mohalla was the worst hit. Every household lost two members. One family lost ten. This was the family of Ghulam Ahmad Bhat, an employee in the veterinary department and a village elder, who later took up the village's case and fought till the government accepted that all those killed were innocent civilians. Bhat lost his own son, three nephews and six other relatives — and yet it took him three-and-a-half years of dogged efforts to prove their innocence. Literally, he turned into an ambassador for the massacred village, carrying its grief to the corridors of power in Srinagar and searching for an echo of compassion.

In a dark carpeted room of Bhat's house, the old men of Pazipora gather one by one. They have come to recollect the massacre, and once more to mourn for their dead. The women sit on the other side of the room, listening to their men in silence. A boy passes a samovar and pours out cups of steaming salt tea. Several of the men puff on a hookah, passing it on. Bhat, sitting in a corner, begins to retell the familiar story. It is a tale he has recounted a hundred times before.

"On that morning, we were having tea. The children were getting ready for school. But then we heard there had been an army crackdown in a neighbouring village, Dedikote. We asked our children not to leave for school. The army had arrested a militant, who was guiding them to hideouts in the area. We had no inkling that anything was going to happen. We later got to know that the militant had led the army into a trap. As the troops returned from the crackdown, a group of militants had laid an ambush near Dingri, only one kilometre from our village."

It was Friday and there was a namaz congregation. As the army convoy passed, the militants opened fire. It continued for a few minutes, then there was complete silence. But this was only the lull before the storm. "As people started fleeing towards the paddy fields, the army jawans fired wildly from the road above," Bhat recounts. "Soon they got reinforcements from Trehgam. Now the villagers were caught in between. The jawans fired on every object, even the slightest movement in the fields."

"It was *al nafsi, al nafsi* (every man for himself). I too fled. Nobody gave a thought to where they were going. It was like a flood, and everybody floated with the stream. I reached Balipora, a neighbouring hamlet, and entered the house of the *numberdar*, Ghulam Rasool. I got into the first room. I still vividly remember there was a fan whirring on the ceiling. I threw myself flat on the floor. Then they started firing. The glass windows shattered, and a barrage of bullets came into the room. Then they started pounding on the door and trying to break it down. I finally found the courage to stand and open the door. An armyman hit me with a rifle butt on my head, even before asking who I was. I was left alive, but one of my nephews was lying dead in a pool of blood."

As the troops entered the village, they segregated the men from the women. The women were taken to the house of Ahad and Gani Khoja. "We heard wails and cries coming from inside. The jawans took us to the mosque compound and beat us, one by one. They had no bullets left, or they would have kept on firing," Bhat said. "Later we heard what had happened to our women. Three unmarried girls had been raped. This is a sworn secret in the village. We all agreed never to tell anyone, because it would ruin the girls' lives."

"An army officer, a captain who had been to our village before, came and told me they had punished us and even set our village (Pazipora) on fire. 'There is nothing left there, just ashes,' he told me. Then they ordered us to pick up the bodies scattered around, but only those of young men. Of the twelve bodies we could identify, three were children from my family, and one was my own son. One boy, Bashir Ahmad, had sixteen bullets in his right arm. His father had to leave another son's body behind to rush Bashir to the hospital in Srinagar."

Bhat says he had turned into a robot. There were too many deaths to mourn. As if so many killings were not enough, they arrested his other son, Abdul Gaffar, along with two villagers. "One was a radio mechanic, known to almost every armyman in Kupwara. The other was a farmer, not even remotely involved in any militant activity, " he says. But the army, he says, needed scapegoats to hide their crime.

"In the evening, we carried the bodies to nearby Poshpora village where we met an army officer. He asked us to go home, but we were drained. I felt as if there were no life left in my legs. I requested him to free my son, and he promised to let him go the next morning. But it was another three-

and-a-half months before we saw our boys again. The army had claimed that all three were militants, and had shown arms supposedly recovered from them in the FIR lodged with the police."

For the next forty-five days, every government agency came to the village, and Bhat had to repeat his story to many officials and journalists. But as time passed and the incident started to fade from memory, fewer and fewer people asked. General Zaki had claimed the first day that the twelve men killed were militants. By now it was widely believed that all the dead were innocent civilians, but the official position was still that only half of the twenty-four killed were civilians. Bhat decided he had to make sure the truth came out. "We were the victims of crime upon crime — an army attack, rape, the arrest of our boys in a cover-up," he says. "But we were the ones who had to prove our innocence, and it took me three-and-a-half years of relentless struggle to accomplish it."

The government had ordered an inquiry. The deputy commissioner was to conduct the probe, but Bhat says he was scared to visit the village. "I went to his office twenty days in a row, but he never agreed to come. Finally, I met the then divisional commissioner C. Phonsong, and requested him to help. He literally forced the DC to visit our village and complete the inquiry." When his report was finally done, it exonerated every one of the dead.

Bhat followed the report from one office to another, and finally approached General Zaki. "It was difficult to reach him, especially if you had a complaint against a security force unit in your hand. The officials screening visitors would not allow you past the first checkpoint. But I played a trick," he recalls. "I put a J&K government cover on the file and pretended it was official. Finally the report received General Zaki's stamp of approval. After more than three years, we had won the battle. But the real war — to see the culprits punished for their crime and justice done to our dead— has never been fought. It is still a distant dream."

As Ghulam Ahmad Bhat recites the tale of the massacre, an old woman hides her face in her lap. Occasionally she wipes away her tears, but she does not break her silence till Bhat has finished. His story concludes and now everybody in the room can hear her sobs. She is Shah Ded, Bhat's sister-in-law. She is illiterate, but she put all her efforts into getting her son, Bashir Ahmad, a good education. He completed school and joined a professional college but was killed in the massacre even before he could bring his first salary home. Amid sobs, she talks about her son.

"He was the apple of our eye. All of us looked up to him. We saved on our expenses to make him happy and comfortable. But Bashir Ahmad was not a child anymore. He had realised his responsibility by then. That morning he called me and said, '*Aapa aapa pareshan mai gus* (Mother, stop being anxious about me now). This year, I will complete my training and return home once and for all. I hope to get a job immediately. Then I will be coming home every day.'"

Usually, she said, she did not allow her son to come to the village because the situation had worsened. But that day,

Sh... ...wenty-four people massacred by the arr... ...y, she blames herself for having asked him to stay on at home for an extra day of holiday.

Groom quits

PONDICHERRY, (UNI)— Close on the heels of a bridegroom from Katterikuppam disappearing on his wedding day on the fourth of this month, another bridegroom, who was to enter into wedlock with his love, was reported missing.

Police said Manimaran of Solainagar was in love with a girl of Mudaliarpet, something which his parents did not like. However, succumbing to pressure from Manimaran, his parents arranged for the wedding, which was to be solemnised at the Cuddalore Thiruvanthipuram Temple on Monday. Though all arrangements had been made for the marriage, the bridegroom did not turn up at the venue, following which the brother of the bride lodged a complaint with the all women police station, alleging that Manimaran had been concealed by his parents.

she stopped him from going back to Srinagar. "I asked him to stay back for a few more days, and I will always blame myself for that," Shah Ded says. "It is like a scar on my heart that will go away only with my death."

When the military came that day, she asked her son and his cousins to leave immediately for a safer place. He did not agree. He said they would simply lie down on the floor. But when the firing started, he ran in panic. "He rushed towards his uncle Ghulam Ahmad Dar in the paddy fields, but he was killed before reaching there. I cannot forget his face," the woman says sadly. "His hands were ready for the henna and I was dreaming of getting him married. My eyes have lost sight, shedding tears in his memory. It was my misfortune that God took him back in the prime of his youth."

Even years later, the death of her son still weighs so heavy on her mind that it is hard for her to see schoolchildren wearing the same colourful uniforms he once wore. "I go back to the days when he would come home from school with mud or ink spilled all over his uniform. Every corner of this village reminds me of him. At times, I feel I should run away from here because his shadows are everywhere. I long to hear him calling me *aapi*."

And even now, she still dreams that one day, her son's death will be avenged. "I wanted to know why he was killed. I tried to ask the big officers who visited here after the massacre, but the men of the village did not let me talk to them," she says. "I am a mother. Everybody, no matter how big an officer, has a mother. I know they will listen to me. One day justice will be done. My son was innocent. His blood will not go to waste."

THE ECONOMICS OF SATI

■ SAGARIKA GHOSE

In economically backward Satpurva village in Uttar Pradesh, a sati becomes a petition to the state, and the relevant question is not whether it was a suicide or a sati, but whether the village can benefit from this "achievement."

THE ECONOMICS OF SATI

November is a cool month in Bundelkhand. Shreds of moist mist hang over the flat green jowar and fields of lentils. Birds flutter in the trees and in the clumps of flowering bushes that fringe the rocky outcrops and hard stony hills. Neelgai, hazardous for the crops, wander under the tall date palms and tamarind trees. At night, gangs of shaitaans dash between the gulleys and deep gorges around the hills. Armed with cheap guns, they are the evil phantoms of the poor and the violent.

In the early morning, villagers sit out in the watery November sunlight, cupping their hands around steaming glasses of tea. The first tentative spirals of woodsmoke carry the smell of fresh rotis into the air. Bundelkhand, roughly the north Madhya Pradesh, south Uttar Pradesh region, is dacoit country. The Chambal ravines to the west ring out with gunshots. In towns like Banda, bedraggled barefoot youth walk along with hunger in their bellies and firepower slung on their shoulders. Bundelkhand is poverty-stricken and savage, beautiful and touristy in parts. The erotic sculptures of the temples in Khajuraho exist as incidentally ancient pleasures in a sunlit swathe of soporific poverty, pitted catastrophic roads, lined by frayed electricity wires dangling above listlessly grazing, skinny cows. This is one of India's most backward regions, though there are some parts that produce betel leaf and are prosperous. And Satpurva village, eight kilometres from the tehsil town of Charkhari in the Mahoba district of UP, is no different from other Bundelkhand villages.

November 11, 1999 dawned quietly over Satpurva. Maan Saah, a respected village elder, weak and cadaverous after more than a decade of tuberculosis, sat outside his hut drinking tea with visiting relatives. Suddenly, the glass slipped from his hands and he died. As the news spread through the village, his widow, Charan Saah, bathed his feet in water and, as is the custom, then drank the same water and sprinkled some of it on her own body. The villagers busied themselves with preparations for the funeral — purchasing *dhoop* from the grocery shop in neighbouring Imaliya village, organising the *kafan*, contributing wood for the pyre, and arranging to send word to Maan Saah's son working as a daily wager in Delhi. No one properly noticed Charan Saah. They say they glimpsed her here and there, seated amongst a group of widows, talking to the women of the village, walking back into the hut and rustling up the calf's feed. After the pyre had been prepared, Maan Saah's body was carried to the cremation ground along the stony path, through the thorny scrub, about a kilometre away from Maan Saah's hut. After his body began to burn, the men went down to the river to take a bath. They did this because some of them believed that the burning body of a TB patient gives off dangerous germs, and also because it is common practice to bathe after a cremation. The flames from Maan Saah's body, faltering at first, began to crackle fitfully.

All of a sudden, Charan Saah, who was sitting with some women and widows in her hut, stood up and began to run towards the cremation ground. She sped down the main village road, past the paved peepal tree, up the rocky path to sit by Maan Saah's pyre. She slumped by the pyre, clinging to it, as if in a trance. The pyre flamed on. Then Charan Saah stood up and began to walk around the pyre. A young relative, Prahlad, grabbed at her, warning her not to get too close. But she turned on him, Prahlad says, in the incarnation of a devi.

THE ECONOMICS OF SATI

Her eyes were red and her tongue flicked out between her teeth. She was demonic, possessed of shakti and shook his hand away ferociously. As the men bathed in the river, and the women wailed in the hut and others clustered around the cremation ground, Charan Saah threw herself into the fire. The flames, witnesses say, began to roar and blaze in sudden energy. Satpurva village had gained its first sati.

There are instances of earlier satis in the Mahoba region. The widow of Shatrughan Sinha (the landowner who donated the land on which Satpurva is built) is said to have committed sati. The women of Satpurva have often attended the sati mela at the sati chabutra in the nearby village of Magrauta. There are three sati temples in the region: in Jaari, Magrauta and Mahoba town. Thousands have been known to attend the temple melas. A report compiled by representatives from independent women's groups and published in the magazine *Manushi* states that after 1981, the year when a sati was committed in Jaari, melas were held for three consecutive years and the administration even provided buses for devotees.

Perhaps expecting similar festivities, minutes after Charan Saah jumped, a huge crowd gathered. A young widow performed a *parikrama* around the fire. Crowds from Imaliya, Banda and Mahoba streamed in. But by 6 pm, the first police trucks thundered in. The exits and entrances to Satpurva were blocked. Six companies of the Provincial Armed Constabulary (PAC) set up their tents on the village outskirts...some relatives say they were beaten up and all sati-related rituals and activities

The police guard the sati sthal in Satpurva village in the immediate aftermath of the incident.

were determinedly squashed. A few days later, representatives from the All India Democratic Women's Association (AIDWA), National Commission for Women (NCW) and other fact-finding teams arrived to investigate, and amid the babble of conflicting accounts of what really happened to Charan Saah, concluded that the death was probably, as official accounts stated, not a sati but a suicide. Yet at the same time, sati traditions and folklore being as strong as they were in this region, and with the poverty and superstitions of the villages so clearly in evidence, there was a strong possibility that Charan Saah herself may have been influenced by the sati cults, and the *Manushi* report concluded that here was an instance of a "complex interweaving of conservative Hindu beliefs and the desire to capitalise on it for commercial purposes."

THE ECONOMICS OF SATI

Where does the "truth" about Charan Saah lie? It lies, basically, in the poverty of Satpurva. In the unpredictable crops, barely enough for subsistence of the village, and which are sometimes ruined by marauding neelgai. Under the treacherous black mud that churns on the dirt track between Satpurva and the main road. In the face of the dirty child who scrabbles in the muddy courtyard of his hut, playing with dung instead of toys. In the murky web of village and family politics where a woman might be gently pressurised to perform the ultimate sacrifice for her husband. In the arms of the man who carried his dying father to a hospital, stumbling on the mud to the highway, only to be told at the hospital that his father was already dead. Or perhaps the truth lies, simply, in the love between Charan Saah and her husband, whom she nursed for almost sixteen years and without whom she was unable to face the thought of living. There are no easy answers, instead there is only a deepening cave of shadows, where voices come echoing out, contradicting and agreeing at the same time. One thing is certain. In a landscape of phantoms, ghosts, evil spirits, fasts and proliferating little religious cults, superstition thrives busily. Faced with the lack of a cash income, of employment opportunities, day after day of battling the elements with very little help from the scientific achievements of modern India, the residents of Satpurva are deadened to human life. The loss of life, by suicide or by murder or by sati, is an act of God, or due to an individual being possessed of shakti or simply the working of fate. They watch as death comes, doing nothing to prevent it or hasten it. They simply watch and wait to see if there's any benefit in it for them afterwards. An important point about Charan Saah's fatal

38

THE ECONOMICS OF SATI

leap was that nobody tried to stop her or pull her back from the flames. Not a single family member or neighbour appeared to believe that she was doing something wrong or superstitious. They simply, fatalistically, watched and accepted her actions as the semi-divine, semi-insane actions of a bereaved woman recently visited by the bewildering immutable powers of death.

A year after Charan Saah's immolation, the villagers of Satpurva are now hopeful for a sati temple. When cash is blindingly inaccessible, when a source of funds seems totally unattainable, then a sati becomes a cottage industry.

"See our village," says Shyam Saah, a resident, "see what a pathetic condition it is in. There is nothing here. No development. Nothing." Although equipped with a handpump and a primary school, the conditions in Satpurva are miserable. Yet it is no extraordinary misery. Satpurva's is the misery seen ordinarily in the outskirts of mofussil towns and in the innumerable villages across India, still untouched by the economic reforms or by the dazzling changes in the metropolitan cities. Its poverty is not hopelessly abject, rather it is frighteningly ordinary. It is the poverty that lives cheek by jowl with the metros, yet is surrealistically untouched by the valuations of dotcoms and the advertisements for the latest cars. It is the poverty that is apparent, ubiquitous, it exists in that space where the city centres inevitably taper off, it boils on the peripheries of every citadel of the new economy. Every design studio in India might overlook a jhuggi, every television

(Facing page) A woman prays at a sati temple in Mahoba, one of the three such temples in the region. The villagers in Satpurva too want such a temple, hoping it will bring in some money.

39

company might hire peons whose parents have sold a human organ to pay off a debt, every five star hotel might offer perfect Pina Coladas served by ragged waiters in brave turbans with frayed cuffs and trousers that are too short. In Satpurva, nestling at the foot of grey stony hills, surrounded with flat fields, there is an awareness that they live in dreadful conditions. There is also a conviction that nothing much will ever become of them and only the occasional mela, election or sati will enable the young men to work off their excess testosterone and the young women their deeply buried anxieties.

The world of Satpurva is confined to a single, mud-churned central road, with the huts and some brick houses arranged in two straight lines on opposite sides of the road. A paved peepal tree stands at the centre of the village. Beyond the peepal, up a rocky path, is the cremation ground. The village fields stretch out in front of the village, running along the bumpy *kuchcha* road to the highway. Inside the cool dark huts, calves bleat next to babies and village women in nylon sarees and bright bindis clutch filthy naked infants. Fevers, malaria and diarrhoea occur regularly, in season, although the village is occasionally visited by a health worker as well as by a *lekhpal* or the keeper of the land register. All of Satpurva's inhabitants are Dalits or Chamars and most of them are *data panthis*. *Data panthis* believe in a guru rather than in conventional Hindu deities, are mostly vegetarian, and encouraged to believe in progressive ideals such as the harmony of all religions. There is no village industry. No handicrafts, supplementary incomes from dairy or poultry farms or trade in wood. Families tear out food from the earth. For cash, they have to migrate to the cities to work either on construction

THE ECONOMICS OF SATI

sites or as domestic servants. "If you had to wake up every morning and go and wash the dishes in somebody else's house, think how low your head would be bowed," says Bind Gopal Bharti, a village resident.

Maan Saah's family, consisting of his two sons, Shishupal and Madanpal and their wives, lives in a mud hut with a few small rooms which it shares with its animals and brood of children. There is not enough land, so young men have to go to Delhi or Kanpur to work as wage labourers. "*Yahan kuch nahin hai,*" says Bijrani, a mother of five, "*kuch nahin. Rasta bhi nahin hai, paani bhi nahin hai, hospital bhi nahin hai.*" Maan Saah's family couldn't afford to admit him to a hospital. Instead, his wife provided him all the welfare she could. She fed him, clothed him, bathed him and gave him whatever medicines they could afford. In the blinding monsoon, when shafts of cold rain beat down into their house, Charan Saah would cover him with all her sarees to keep him from fever.

The exact circumstances of the incident are shrouded in confusion. Some villagers confirm Maan Saah died in the morning, others insist he died the previous night. Some say the police beat up many villagers, others say there were no beatings. Some say Charan Saah was at home when the pyre was lit and somehow knew exactly when it was kindled and then began to run. Others say she had been at the cremation ground from the beginning. The women's organisations say that because Charan Saah was not dressed in bridal finery, there was no prior plan of immolation. She was suffering from a "depressive suicidal syndrome," they say, and see it as a case of suicide and not sati. The villagers, on the other hand, protest that it is unfair not to call it a sati. The laughable paradox is that while hopeful outsiders conclude that Charan Saah was not in fact a victim of obscurantism and pressure, the villagers appear to insist on their right to be obscurantist! They see the attempt to deny them of their sati achievement as a denial of their due rights.

Shishupal is a quiet, unassuming man who doesn't know why his mother immolated herself but today, he and his family

Charan Saah's son, Shishupal (extreme left) with other family members. "What's the point of all this news coverage...if we don't get anything out of it?"

THE ECONOMICS OF SATI

are anxious that her sacrifice be recognised. "At least if we get a temple, we'll get some money and there might be some benefit for our village." When Charan Saah was burning at the pyre, at some point her body apparently fell out of the flames. But the *lekhpal*, one Santram Khushwaha, urged the villagers to push the body back in and rekindle the fire. The *Manushi* report quotes him as saying, "Now she is dead, let her body burn properly. Put more cow dung cakes in the fire. If she is regarded as having committed sati then the whole village will benefit materially. The village will get a road and other development benefits if there is a sati." Vishwanath, another resident, says he had heard that in Rajasthan, in Rajput villages, once a sati takes place, there's tremendous progress and that water, roads and electricity are provided. "Now that we have a sati, we too should get these benefits," he says. A year after the sati, it is seen as a chillingly pragmatic developmental initiative.

In the cacophony of voices competing for the government's assistance, the voice that attracts the most attention will, it is assumed, reap at least some rewards. And given the resounding absence of other means of attracting attention, a violent or an abnormal death becomes a petition to the state. It becomes an application form, a means of finding a place in the government's sun. Poverty, as Amartya Sen has written, is not simply the lack of income. It is also the lack of a voice, of a responsive local administration that can redress local needs, the lack of a system of governance that is transparent and accountable to the people it supposedly exists to serve. In the absence of all these factors, in a situation where political and economic poverty feed off each other, the actual facts about Charan Saah's death become almost immaterial. The reasons why she gave up her life matter not a jot among villagers who have at last found a pretext for getting outsiders to become interested in their village. Every villager knows that had it not been for Charan Saah, Satpurva would be just another boringly pathetic statistic in some crumbling record book in a district headquarter. They all know that if they were to propagate the information that there was nothing "abnormal" about the death, that it was just another routine suicide, Satpurva's saliency, however dubious and short-lived, would be destroyed.

Whether or not Charan Saah committed suicide or sati, whether her act was born out of pressure or was entirely voluntary, whether or not she was ill-treated by her sons and decided to die because she could not face life as a Dalit widow in a village without enough land, whether it was her undying love for her husband that made her scornful of a fiery end, whether she was mentally disturbed and suffering from hysteria, a year later all of these are simply irrelevant details for the villagers. All they care about is the investiture of sati "status" on their village and the grant of money to build a temple. "What does it matter if it was a sati or a suicide?" Shishupal asks. "It doesn't matter to her. She is dead. But we are alive and we should get the benefits. What is the point of all this news coverage? What is the point of all these people coming to our village if we don't get anything out of it?" Shishupal believes that the reason why the administration is forcibly preventing the construction of a temple in Satpurva, given the fact that there are other sati temples in the area, is because this is a Dalit village and Charan Saah was a Dalit woman. Sati is a practice reserved for the nobility, for the ranis or for upper-

THE ECONOMICS OF SATI

caste Brahmin and Kshatriya women. When a Dalit commits sati, the administration refuses to give it any importance.

The women of Satpurva are equally emphatic. "Who knows when the shakti will come to a woman?" asks Ramkali. "After all, it takes courage to jump into the fire and those who do it, should be worshipped." There is a certain feminine machismo. "Look at her power," says a woman neighbour. "She was stronger than most men. Would a man ever jump live into the fire?" Other women say that as soon as they heard that a sati had been performed, they just grabbed their children and rushed to see it. "Everyone likes to see a brave woman die," says Ramkali. "The kind of courage she showed, even a maharani would not show." Manu Prasad Tiwari, a guide at the Jain temple in Khajuraho, says that once a woman has decided to commit a sati nothing can stop her. You can bind her in chains in a police lock-up but the chains will begin to bleed and she will run to the fire. You can try to stop her but she will kill you if she must in order to perform her duty.

But isn't this *andhvishwas*, terribly backward thinking in a democracy where all citizens have a right to life as individuals, not as wives or widows? "Rubbish!" explodes Tiwari. "The world has gone mad today. Which child properly knows his scriptures? Which child is able to recite the Vedas? Why do children call their parents mummy and daddy when they should refer to them as mataji and pitaji. We are losing our *sanskriti*. In these circumstances, if a woman chooses to commit sati, she should be praised and worshipped as one who is taking care to abide by our ancient traditions. You can't judge everyone by your own standards. Perhaps she did it because she wanted to enjoy heavenly paradise. Be united with her husband. A sati is truly a noble woman."

Sitting in front of the blue-painted mud walls of her hut, Javitri performs a small puja to a fertility cult. On a steel dish are arranged a bunch of leaves smeared with *sindoor*, some *suparis* and a small clay idol. Next to her hut, a rivulet of slush runs with garbage and dog excrement. A group of young women crowd around her as she performs a small *mannat* for her family's crops. One of the women, Bindu, dressed in a bright pink sari with blazing *sindoor* in her hair, stares with blank resentment. "No good will come to anyone from anything," she shrugs, bored and tired. "Yes, some girls go to school. No, not many of them complete school. Yes, some men get an education. No, they don't get jobs. Everywhere there is *bekaari* and *berozgaari*. What good is an education? Better to learn a language and speak to the foreigners and get money from them. In Khajuraho, there are people who can speak French and German, they do well. What is the point of studying? Those who open motorcycle repair shops, they do well. I don't want to leave this village. What will I do in the city? Live in a jhuggi and clean somebody else's toilet? I don't think there's anything wrong with sati. In our religion we refer to all women as satis. We refer to men and women as Purush and Sati. If the police had not stopped it, we would have got a temple and a *chadhona* of more than one lakh."

THE ECONOMICS OF SATI

At the sati temple in Mahoba, one of the priest's assistants says that most of the sati temples that exist in the area commemorate satis committed by upper-caste women. The Mahoba mandir, built in the thirties under huge overhanging trees, is a crumbling moss-covered building with an indeterminate idol of a woman at the centre, daubed with peeling paint. A few stringy marigold garlands are draped across the idol and stray dogs and cows wander in the muddy compound. Past the building, the land slopes to a small stream. Children run about on its banks and chuck stones and leaves on the water. A few ten paise and twenty paise coins — currency that cannot be used in any Indian city — lie forlornly on the small square of paved earth in front of the idol. The priest says sati temples are no longer at the height of their glory and people's faith in sati is diminishing because of outside influences.

Not many frequent the Mahoba temple nowadays, although there was once a fairly good road connecting it to the highway and the settlement near the temple was called the "sati mohalla." The sati temple at Jaari, constructed in 1981 to commemorate the sati of an eighteen-year-old Brahmin widow, also no longer attracts many devotees. In fact, the priest says, lower castes visit Jaari far more than the upper castes, although the mela is no longer as grand as it used to be for fear of the police and their beatings. "The upper castes don't need sati anymore. They get their money from somewhere or another. But the lower castes still think that maybe they can get money and benefits from sati. But there is an overwhelming fear of the police. That is what is stopping sati from being as popular as it used to be."

As in most social practices, sati has always had a material

inspiration. The claims of a widow on a husband's property and assets have traditionally been regarded as a destabilising factor in families. A young and attractive widow might also become the object of desire for other male members of the family and there may be a breakdown in community relations because of her. An unattached "tainted" woman is not only a financial but also a moral liability. Thus sati is an efficient way of sorting out the dead man's legacy as well as maintaining the family status quo. Nowadays, since a widow can become an economic agent by becoming employed, her ability to generate cash on her own can be taken as a somewhat adequate compensation for the fact that her husband's economic potential has ceased to exist. But the fact that the practice of sati is banned, and is therefore rare, has transformed it into a grand scale soap opera not only for the mainstream media but for the local inhabitants. It has also come to be regarded as an activity with high possibilities of income for a large group of people. For the inhabitants of Satpurva, the denial of the economics of sati has become a cause of resentment and sorrow. As Govind Das, another village elder, says, "It's a very sad thing, the way Charan Saah died. Really it was very sad. We felt bad, but at least now that it is over, we should get some development."

Says Charan Saah's son Shishupal: "Sati, suicide, I don't know what it was. My parents are dead. For years my father suffered and my mother looked after him. She was a strong woman. She supervised the house and the grandchildren. I don't know what happened to her. She loved him a lot. These are all individual decisions. I don't know what is in someone else's mind. They don't know what is in my mind. *Sab alag alag hote hai*. Every human being is different. How can I know what was on her mind? But at least a temple...maybe, or perhaps a *chaupal*...maybe some grant or something...?"

Sunsets are slow over Satpurva. First long shadows advance across the fields, like slow dark pythons. Then the white stone hills begin to darken, then the trees become black monoliths, radiating darkness from their leaves, then the cows and bullocks turn homeward and shepherd boys straggle behind them, shouting in the clay lamp twilight. In the dead of night, the shaitaans will roam the fields, villagers will toss with mosquitoes in their sleep and a grandchild will stare dead-eyed at the place where his grandmother once slept and remember how he watched her burn alive. But perhaps he won't think of her death as anything remarkable. He will probably remember his grandmother's leap into the flames as a moment of hope for the elders of the village. He will remember the excited whispered plans among them. And he will remember it as a time when crowds of outsiders armed with cameras, microphones, papers and pens, and police trucks armed with lathis, turned up at the village, stayed for a few days and then went back to where they had come from, leaving the sun to set on Satpurva as it had done ever since he could remember.

STILL THERE

SANKARSHAN THAKUR

> Ten years after a Chamar boy and a Jat girl were hanged by a Jat-dominated panchayat for eloping, mindsets have not changed in Mehrana village in Uttar Pradesh. The village now has a Chamar sarpanch, but only in name, for the Jats still call the shots.

STILL THERE

Early on the morning of 27 March 1991, two Chamar boys, Brijendra and Ram Kishan, and a Jat girl, Roshni, were hanged to death from a tree in Mehrana, a village on the Uttar Pradesh-Rajasthan border some 130 kilometres southeast of Delhi.

The hanging was ordered by an impromptu panchayat and the sentence was carried out swiftly. It was not a furtive act; it was a public statement. A stirring, thrilling spectacle meant to inspire awe and strike terror, a raucous, almost festive beheading right out of a period film on medieval mores. Only, the little autocracy of Mehrana didn't possess anything quite as sophisticated as a guillotine. They used ropes pulled off the necks of their cattle. The two boys were in their late teens, the girl was fifteen.

The charge against them was that one of the Chamar youngsters, Brijendra, and Roshni had eloped for a few days before returning home to announce that they wished to be man and wife. Ram Kishan was an accomplice in the alleged escapade and an abettor of forbidden love between a Chamar boy and a Jat girl.

Chamars are Harijans of the cobbler caste, hardy untouchables who have subsisted on the fringes of existence, dealing exclusively in the foul business of filth. It has been their job for millennia to wait on dying cattle of the wealthy and clear the carcasses when their owners have no use left for them. That has been their life — hiding dead cattle, then tanning leather and then turning it into footwear for feet that rested on their heads. The Chamar has a status in the Constitution of India and in the speeches of leaders seeking votes, but not at home in the village. He is fed promises but not food. He is hungry, and therefore, a willing slave. Slogans will not douse the hunger in his stomach. Deprivation and despair have killed his spirit, if ever he had any. He is meant to have no pride, no self-esteem, no notion of himself as a human being.

Jats in these parts, and in many others, to be sure, tend, by dint of birth, to be masters of all they survey. Just part of the advantage of being a Jat is that your nose is forever in the air. The rest is at your feet: history, custom, community, the law, even the state and its many well-meaning instruments which have so often wilted to Jat tyranny, or to that of their more twisted, more macho, upper-caste brethren, the Thakurs.

The police made arrests after the outrage of Mehrana rippled into public view. More than fifty Mehrana villagers, most of them upper-caste elders, were taken in but they were all let off quietly once that capricious thing called public attention roved away from Mehrana. The cases were never pursued. The culprits of 1991 roam free.

Why, is a question that throws up no definite answers. Hearsay abounds. Some say the Jats paid off the Chamar elders to get the cases withdrawn, others that there was a formal out-of-court settlement; the Chamars had neither the money nor the will to push ahead with the prosecution, they settled for a bit of under-the-table pelf. The Chamars, of course, deny receiving any payoffs and the Jats deny offering them. But whatever the finer detail, the Jats were able to use money or influence or both to manoeuvre the system that in any case works for them — the police, the local administration, the politicians.

STILL THERE

The Mehrana hangings came at a handy time for the Jats. It was the eve of the 1991 general elections and no politician wanted to risk being at the wrong end of Jat opinion. The Chandra Shekhar government was too dominated by Jats to have bothered doing anything. The Congress party, then the crutch that held up Chandra Shekhar in power, had its own share of Jat bigwigs not wanting to annoy the community — Natwar Singh, who came from nearby Bharatpur, Balram Jakhar, Avtar Singh Badhana. They wanted to shed no tears. The Congress did send a delegation to Mehrana but it went almost undercover. Meira Kumar, daughter of the great Chamar patriarch Babu Jagjivan Ram, made the trip on behalf of the Congress, promised to take up the Chamars' case and returned to Delhi to promptly forget about Mehrana. The balance of votebanks in west Uttar Pradesh and Rajasthan did not favour the Congress speaking on behalf of the Chamars. So they were only being politically correct.

I grew up in times and places where the caste system was part of the natural order of things. And what goes by the name of caste atrocity — excesses committed by the upper castes on lower castes in exercise of their divine rights — was so commonplace that it did not even fetch notice. It was much, much later that I realised, for instance, that Ramesraa and Munesraa, the obliging djinns of my childhood fancies, the tireless workhorses of my north Bihar village home, were actually Rameshwar and Muneshwar. But they were never to be afforded the dignity of being called by their given names.

They were both lowborn. They could not even have proper names. And if they did, those names had to be phonetically thrashed out of resemblance to the original. Rameshwar and Muneshwar are both synonyms of God. How would the highborn ever beckon the lowborn by the name of God? Their names had to be converted, perverted, squeezed of all dignity.

Strong intonations of colloquialism and dialect do dwell in the speech of Bihar but I have never come across a highborn Rameshwar being called Ramesraa. They would be Ramesarji, or Ramesar, never Ramesraa, never that disdainful long vowel dragging the name at the end. I have a feeling Ramesraa, smiling serf though he remained all his life, discerned this sneer in the way their names were pronounced. He resorted to a quiet, docile little revolt. He called his son Junglee, the wild one. No Sanskritisation, nothing to do with the gods, nothing that could be distorted, or needed to be.

I called Rameshwar Ramesraa and Muneshwar Munesraa without realising my tongue was an instrument of an age-old perversion, minor though it was compared to some of the other things that were happening in the years that shaped the consciousness of my generation. Belchi and Piparia, Arwal and Masaurhi, Sarhupur and Deoli, blister after bloody blister, but always the same story screaming from different datelines: wanton, unpunished rape, murder and pillage by those who had upon those who hadn't.

The victims of Sarhupur and Deoli in 1981 and the victims of Mehrana ten years on, were the same: poor, woebegotten Chamars, Harijans, the children of God and the slaves of their earthly *mai-baaps*, the highborn, the upper castes. Twenty-three Harijans were gunned down in Sarhupur by Thakurs. In Deoli, henchmen of Brahmin and Thakur landlords carried fire through a Harijan basti, killing a dozen and burning their entire colony down to ashes. The Brahmins and the Thakurs here, the Bhumihars there, and even, in places, the Yadavs who, being the latest entrants to the oppressors' club, were often the harshest, the most zealous exploiters. They drenched season after season with stains that remain, or should, on the tattered conscience of the nation. Sarhupur and Deoli were, in fact, not far from Mehrana. Just across the Sher Shah Suri Marg, or the Grand Trunk Road, the dorsal flank of the arid, unchanging wilderness that is the junction of Uttar Pradesh and Rajasthan.

So when Mehrana happened in 1991, it shocked but it didn't surprise. It shouldn't have happened but such things just did. It was like disease — abhorrent but existent, part of life.

When I reached Mehrana the morning after the hangings in March 1991, the entire village gathered to tell me that what had happened had to happen, that what had happened was right. Stringing three teenagers up a tree and throttling the life out of them was not a symptom of any disease but a prescription for cure. The age-old village order had been violated, it had to be restored. Strong medicine was needed; strong medicine had been administered. The Jats held the ramparts; the Chamars cowered in their mental dungeons, not even able to freely mourn lest they provoked

The author in Mehrana the morning after the hangings in March 1991 — "Mehrana was not remorseful that day, but pulsing with a sense of achievement, as if it had put down an insurrection."

Jat ire. Mehrana was not remorseful. Mehrana was pulsing with a sense of achievement, as if they had put down an insurrection. Which they had, in a manner of speaking. Marriage between Brijendra and Roshni would have meant a mutiny against Jat hegemony.

■

> *The lawyer stood by the thesis of homicide...and the twins declared at the end of the trial that they would have done it again a thousand times over for the same reason. It was they who gave a hint of the direction the defence would take as soon as they surrendered to their church a few minutes after the crime. They burst panting into the parish house, closely pursued by a group of roused-up Arabs, and they laid the knives, with clean blades, on Father Amador's desk. Both were exhausted from the barbarous work of death, and their clothes and arms were soaked and their faces smeared with sweat and still living blood.*
>
> *"We killed openly," Pedro Vicario said, "but we are innocent."*
>
> *"Perhaps before God," said Father Amador.*
>
> *"Before God and before men," Pablo Vicario said, "It was a matter of honour."*
>
> — From *Chronicle of a Death Foretold*, by Gabriel Garcia Marquez

So it must have been for the Jats of Mehrana too. A matter of honour.

Marquez wrote *Chronicle of a Death Foretold* half a world

across from Mehrana and more than a decade before Mehrana happened. Long years after he finished it, he told friend and fellow Latin writer Plinio Mendoza in the course of a long conversation on his life and work that he abhorred fantasy, that all his fiction was, in fact, fact. "...imagination is just an instrument for producing reality. The source of creation is always, in the last instance, reality." Marquez's fiction was Mehrana's fact. One was like the other's umbra — fact and fiction, refractions of the same essentials of nature and reality: prejudice, pride, bigotry, love, hatred, honour, vengeance, violence.

The Chamar boys had had the temerity to not only look a Jat girl in the eye but also to court her, to elope with her. They had, as the panchayat put it, committed an *"asahya kukarm"* — an intolerable misdeed. It was for the Jats more than a mere matter of honour; it was a threat to their carefully preserved myth of superiority, an alarming trespass into their domain. If the Chamar was allowed to do what the Jat had been doing for centuries, it could be the beginning of the end of his dominion. The boys had to die. More than punishment, their hanging was meant to be another lesson scorched on a defeated psyche.

But why did Roshni, born to Jats, have to die? Because she had an uncomfortable truth to tell? Perhaps. But besides that, she too had committed a crime beyond forgiving — she had allowed the untouchable boy more than just a touch. Worse, she had defended her liaison with Brijendra rather than disown him. That would have been easy to do; all it required was for Roshni to have said she had been forced away by Brijendra, that it was abduction, not elopement. But Roshni stood by Brijendra; the Jats had to disown her.

The first thing the Jats did after deciding to kill was to try and absolve themselves of the crime they were about to commit. When the Jats wove their escape route by rigging a panchayat on the morning of 27 March and getting it to accept their decision as its own — and, therefore, of all Mehrana — nobody even so much as stirred a finger in protest; they didn't dare. When Mangtu Pahalwan, Jat elder and village landlord, rose to declare: "I am the *daroga*, I am the *tehsildar*, I am the judge," nobody stood up in challenge. When the ruling pantheon — the Pahalwan, Mukhiya Nawal Singh, Nirtu, Pritam, Tulsi Ram and other Jat elders — decreed death, most clapped and some merely hung their heads in mute assent. Inder Sain Jatav was among them and his few, halting words told you why they got away with it. "We have never looked the Jats in the eye, that is not the custom. When I was a child, my father used to tell me they would take my eyes out if I did that...."

Inder Sain Jatav watched the hanging in silence, all the village Chamars watched it. It was, after all, a show put up essentially for them, wasn't it? So they would be reminded of the dos and don'ts, of what the Jats could do if you looked them in the eye and what they could do if you touched their women.

The law arrived when custom was finished with its statement. One of the jawans of Uttar Pradesh's Provincial Armed Constabulary, which pulled into Mehrana with some of us the morning after, told me, "They had to die for what they did. You and I may not like it and you and I will both write reports about it, but they had to die. *Yehi gaon ki reet hai*, this is the way of the village...."

But that happened a long time back, in the bygone century. The world has changed since then, or so we tell ourselves day after day. Change is the charioteer of our fast-forwarded times. Things change, and before we can grasp them, things change again. In the years since the Mehrana hangings, the face of the world has morphed. Unseen curtains on the map have collapsed in heaps and boundaries and colours have changed. Empires have expired and markets have blossomed. The Internet has arrived and placed progress on a new super speedway; the whole wide world is in the grip of the web. India has become a nuclear power. And a Chamar has become the sarpanch of Mehrana.

Chamartola, 1991: The huts lie clustered in a hollow dustbowl at the edge farthest from the village pond and the water tank. The small frontages are swept clean but the insides are dark and dank. A group of Chamar elders sit in the little clearing of Chamartola, wrapped in rancid shawls, silently puffing on the dying embers of an earthen hookah. Their children and their pigs squeal about them. Their women are huddled behind a mud wall like a gaggle of grimy geese, all on their haunches, their sarees pulled long over their faces, sobbing collectively. This isn't grief they can be demonstrative about; the Jats won't take kindly to that. In the distance, further away from the village and closer to the bush, a pyre smoulders. "Where did these boys get such ideas, why did they have to start behaving like the Jats?" mutters one of the old men irritably, "Didn't they know they would end up like this? Slaves should learn to live like slaves."

Chamartola, 2000: When Sarpanch Gangaram walks from one part of Mehrana to the other, he does not walk through the village of which he is now the elected chief. He goes right round the outer perimeter. Sarpanch Gangaram is an old and feeble man. He says he is fifty-five but he looks a rather weather-beaten seventy-five, his cheeks pulled in on his facial bones, his back bent like a birch in high wind. It would save him a lot of bother taking the short route through the village streets. But he hobbles round the elaborate belt on his bamboo staff, as if he were barred entry to Mehrana.

Sarpanch Gangaram admits he is a sarpanch only in name. "To one acre of our land they (the Jats) have forty. Do you know the meaning of the weight of forty acres of land sitting on one? Their cattle eat better stuff than us."

I asked him that and he mildly protested. "No, no, not that, this is just old habit. From my childhood we were taught never to crisscross the village too often, the Jats never liked us doing that...it is just an old habit. I am used to it."

But surely all that has changed now? This is the twenty-first century and he is the sarpanch?

"Oh, I could go and nobody would stop me. Nothing will happen to me, I can go. But this is just an old habit, why change settled ways? I will prove nothing by walking through Mehrana, what will be the point? There are no rules about these things, there is just a custom and we live by it."

We were sitting in front of Sarpanch Gangaram's house in the dustbowl on the edge of the village. "Gangaram?" one of the village boys had asked when I had sought directions to where the sarpanch of Mehrana lived. He had waved his arm in the general direction of Chamartola before turning and sauntering off disinterestedly. *"Baahar, baahar, gaon ke peechhe"* (Outside, outside, behind the village).

Chamartola hadn't changed. Gangaram's house was two shacks roofed over with dried twigs and a little portmanteau courtyard — pigsty, playground, shed, barn, kitchen, latrine, sit-out, bedroom, the sarpanch's court. All around it lay the abandon and disarray of poverty: refuse heaps, choked drains spilling over, drowsy dogs, emaciated cattle, cold stoves, filth, stench, naked grime-ridden children, wailing.

When he emerged from his black hole in the wall, Gangaram was in nothing but a piece of cloth that concealed his privates. His person exhaled belligerent fumes of damp tobacco and sweat. As sarpanch he may well have turned back an unannounced caller but I had counted on his comprehension of his lowly status. A Chamar would not turn back a visitor from the city; he wouldn't have the social confidence to do that, his genes wouldn't give him the guts, sarpanch or no sarpanch. The poor don't lock their doors — often they don't have doors to lock — and they don't keep appointment diaries. Gangaram went back in as quickly as he came out, but that was only because his countenance had embarrassed him. He came out again a few minutes later, straightening his crumpled kurta and dhoti and smiling an uncertain smile behind his folded hands. "Is anything wrong?" he asked, "Is anything the matter?"

A crowd had slowly gathered and Gangaram, relieved that I wasn't any agent of adverse news, had ordered his cot out into the courtyard. He was also trying, step by step, to fit the description of sarpanch. He had asked one of the boys to fetch a pack of bidis from the corner shop, pulling out a ten-rupee note from his pocket rather importantly. He had got his daughter to bring him his bamboo staff. He had also asked for his pugree but his wife sent word back from inside that there was no pugree; there never had been one. His wife shouted from inside the room and the tone of her words suggested surprise and irritation at her husband's sudden request. Gangaram was left embarrassed a second time but he made as if he hadn't heard; he waved his staff in the manner of a sceptre and motioned the crowd to scatter. Nobody did; they only closed in further around his cot. They were jostling, giggling, urging Gangaram to look the part — to sit straighter, to hold his staff this way or that, to get a shine on his worn *juttis*. If this was a court, Gangaram could only qualify as its jester.

Nothing that Gangaram wore or did added up to the image of a sarpanch. He didn't even have a full-time hanger-on. I asked him where he worked out of and he didn't get the question. I asked him where the panchayat met and he said, "We have to decide that. The Chaudharys (the Jat elders) haven't called a meeting yet, when they call a sitting of the panchayat I will go."

Some of the youngsters in the gathering started laughing derisively at this. Embarrassment spread on Gangaram's helpless face yet again. "You see, I have been elected sarpanch because this year this seat was reserved for the scheduled castes. The Jats could not put up a candidate, otherwise who could have defeated them?"

"*Arre, inke paas to sarpanch ka stamp bhi nahin hai*," a voice in the crowd added, "*robe to Jaaton kaa hi hai, sarpanch hamare Gangaramji hain aur pradhani karenge Jat*" (This man does not even possess the seal of the sarpanch. The Jats are still all-powerful. Gangaram is the sarpanch but the real bosses are the Jats).

It sounded like Gangaram was being mocked. But in truth the anonymous speaker at the back of the crowd was only trying to explain Gangaram's unenviable lightness of being. He was sarpanch but not even a dummy — he didn't have an office, he hadn't called a meeting, he was not even required to put his seal of approval on a decision taken by others. He was just there, a sarpanch without a panchayat, as it were. If his people laughed at Gangaram acting the sarpanch, it was not because they meant him any disrespect. They weren't laughing at Gangaram, they were laughing at the sheer meaninglessness of his being sarpanch, they were laughing at themselves. Any

Chamar sarpanch would be a laughing matter. The voice appeared to have stated all that Gangaram wanted to state but was embarrassed to tell. "That is about all the truth," he said, splaying his palms, "I am sarpanch for a year, the Jats have ruled for centuries. We have to live with them, what do you expect of me?" Could one village election, superimposed by a quota system that would switch villages at the end of the term, turn history? Could Gangaram turn the future?

"How?" he asked, "With what? To one acre of our land, they have forty. Do you know the meaning of the weight of forty acres of land sitting on one? Their cattle eat better stuff than us."

Sarpanch Gangaram was a witness to the hangings of March 1991. Of course, he was then just Gangaram Chamar, not sarpanch. But would that have made a difference? "We could do nothing, nothing," he said, speaking only reluctantly about what had happened a decade ago. "They later said we all had endorsed the panchayat's decision, all the Chamars. Could we have, in our hearts? But did we have an option?"

So I asked him if there could be a repeat of 1991 in Mehrana. Could that happen again, in the new century, under a Chamar sarpanch? Gangaram lowered his head on his staff and pondered and then said something that was numbing in its depth of meaning: "Our boys will never commit such a mistake again." It was not for the sarpanch to offer any guarantees on what the Jats might or might not do. It was for the sarpanch only to state that his people had taken the lesson of the hangings to heart.

Jatmohalla, 1991: The narrow lane leading up from Chamartola twists and turns and opens into a wide space from where more of the sky is visible. The huts have given way to concrete structures. Their huge timber and iron gates open on cobbled pathways leading up to the havelis where linger the signs of plenty: motorcycles, tractors, sackfuls of grain that come from the acres they plough, labourers loading and unloading the fresh harvest. Half a dozen men sitting on the verandah of Mangtu Pahalwan's house smoke from an ornate hookah with a brass pipe and holder. The police are all over the village ostensibly looking for the "culprits behind the crime" but they seem relaxed, unperturbed. "So you've been talking to those Chamars," says one of a group of Jat youngsters hanging about Mangtu Pahalwan's house. Their tone is taunting, almost accusatory. "So what took you to the Chamars first? And what tales of misery have they been feeding you?" There are half a dozen of them, lounging in the sun. "If you would care to note down our statement too, write," the boy continues, "We would like to tell you that what happened was right and just and it will happen again if those bloody untouchables dare to cross our path and touch our women. Our blood boils at the thought of a Chamar touching our women, now these fellows won't dare."

Jatmohalla, 2000: Mangtu Pahalwan was asleep, he could not be disturbed. "What is the matter anyhow?" asked the man who later turned out to be a manager of the Pahalwan's estates. "He has just had lunch and he usually sleeps a while." He said I could wait if I wished so I waited on the Pahalwan's verandah watching his buffaloes chew cud.

It was a hot afternoon and the lanes of Jatmohalla were

empty save for the buffaloes. After a while, the manager appeared again and asked what it was that I wanted to meet the Pahalwan about and I told him it was about the hangings of 1991. "Oh," he said in almost a sigh of surprise and vanished.

When Mangtu Pahalwan finally came, swatting invisible flies with a *gamchha*, he pretended as if the hangings were an obscure event that he was having problems locating in the deep, hazy past: "*Haan, haan, wo jo ghatana hui thhi...lekin uska kya? Ab to sab kuchh theek thaak hai, jo beet gayi, so baat gayi*" (Oh yes, that incident...but what about it? Everything is in order now. What is past is forgotten).

He wouldn't talk about it unless he knew he had no choice. He asked me if I was a policeman. Then he asked me if I was the new local magistrate. Finally he asked me if someone, someone important, from Delhi had sent me. And when he was convinced I was only a scribe with nothing more than a pen and a notebook he felt bold enough to say he had nothing to say: "*Gade murde kyon ukharte ho? Woh us samay ki baat thhi, eeshwar ki leela thhi, ghat gayi*" (Why do you pick on old issues? It was something that happened a long time back, it was an act of God, it happened).

So I asked him if he had no remorse at what had happened, if he really thought it was an act of God. "*Jab pratha todi jaati hai to kisi na kisi ko dand bhugatna padta hai*," he said and rose to leave. (When customs are broken someone has to pay the price.) His tone was firm and he seemed to believe what he was saying. It was an act of God, he had been an instrument of God, he had meted out natural, if not divine, justice.

It could happen again, then, I asked him, as I had asked Sarpanch Gangaram. "This is a question you should ask

Gangaram. He is the sarpanch now, he will tell you what can happen and what cannot," the Pahalwan said and ended the meeting.

The Tree, 1991: Its growth has been stunted, for it rises between the tumbling tomb of a nameless pir and a shrine to Shiva. It lacks the girth of a banyan, though a banyan it is; its trunk is typically gnarled and its shoots are drooping to the ground from its branches. It looks fragile at the top but it took the weight of three bodies hanging from it. When they had been swung up and down repeatedly, like weights on a pulley, the bodies were laid on the ground. "We didn't know the mechanics of hanging people so we kept pulling the bodies up and down like we do with buckets in a well, till we were sure," a Jat boy who sat through the proceedings says. His eyes are lit up with excitement and pride, as if he were relating a great moment. But Brijendra and Roshni, so most villagers say, were still alive when their bodies were brought down from the tree. But the panchayat was in a hurry. The bodies of the two were dragged — "like a dog drags a carcass" — down to the pond nearby. "When the pyre was ready," says the Jat boy, "the whole village resounded with *jayjaykaar*."

The Tree, 2000: The Tree is still there. Its trunk has aged and its roots have clawed into the earth more firmly. I had half

(Facing page) The tree from which the three youngsters were hanged is still there, a symbol of what could still happen to the Chamars if they dared challenge Jat hegemony.

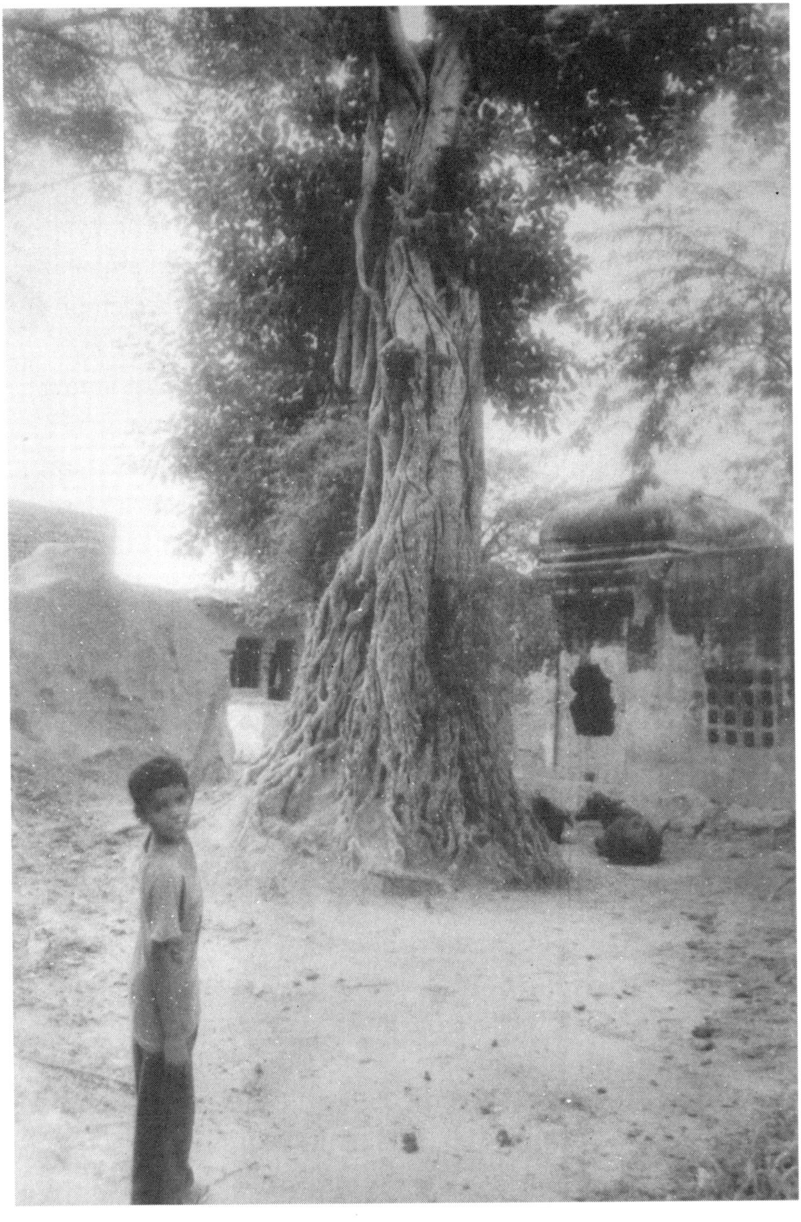

expected the tree to have gone, slaughtered by the villagers as an act of obliterating a memory that they had no wish to preserve. But the tree is still there. So are some proud raconteurs of its role in Mehrana's recent history. They want it preserved, not as a reminder of what cannot be repeated but of what should not be repeated. When people pass the tree it probably tells them what they cannot and must not do, it probably draws the line for them, it probably is preserved as the defining line of hegemonies.

The little boy who ran ahead in the dust excitedly pointing out the tree — "This is it, here it is, this is the tree from which they were hanged, the three of them!" — could not even have been conceived when the hangings of March 1991 took place. He was barely seven. Yet he knew everything. He had been told everything, down to each detail. He even pointed out the branches from which the bodies had been hanged, leaping, jumping, pointing his fingers as he ran round and round the banyan tree.

Myth and lore live in the minds of generations and they are passed on because they serve ends, they are the teller's version of black and white, right and wrong, moral and immoral. It is nowhere written that Mehrana was the paternal home of Yashoda, foster mother of Krishna. Nandgaon, Krishna's paternal home, is a walk from Mehrana. Other ports of call in Krishna's worldly itinerary — Mathura, Vrindaban, Goverdhan — are all in the near distance. There is nowhere any proof that there was once a Lord called Krishna who had a foster mother called Yashoda. That he had a brute of an uncle called Kansa, ruler of Mathura, and that Nand crossed the big flood to place the newborn Krishna in the safe custody of Yashoda. But Krishna is an elaborate, intricately fashioned myth that has come down generation after generation. It has become faith. There was Krishna and he had a foster mother called Yashoda whose paternal home was a village called Mehrana.

It is also nowhere written, other than in scraps of newspapers that were recycled long back, that Brijendra and Ram Kishan and Roshni were hanged on a banyan tree on the banks of the village pond. The little boy who became my guide to the tree could only have heard the story. And to know it so well, he must have heard it several times. So the story is being told. It is being passed on to generations. New myth is in the process of being made to buttress that most durable and indestructible of our myths — the myth of caste superiority.

> *... Once upon a time there lived in the village a wicked and disobedient boy called Brijendra. Brijendra struck a friendship with a beautiful girl called Roshni and, one night, he ran away with her. The entire village was shocked and angry at what had happened. The gods too were very upset because what Brijendra had done was against the order dictated by them. Brijendra was a lowly Chamar and Roshni belonged to a family of Jats. Curses would fall on the village if the villagers did not do something about it. So they called a great panchayat and decided to punish the errant boy and girl for the sin they had committed by going against the divine order. They were hanged and the entire village performed a yagna*

to purify itself. Finally the gods were pleased and the villagers lived happily ever after....

That, in effect, is the story that the children of Mehrana are being told because that is how the little boy related it to me. The boy will turn an adult in the new century and perhaps he too will pass the story — and the moral — of Mehrana's banyan tree on. Like all stories consciously preserved and like all methylated myths, this one too serves ends.

FRAGMENTS FROM A FOLDER

SIDDHARTHA DEB

> Given mainstream India's lack of interest in the North-east, secession for the North-eastern states is simply a ratification of their alien status, an attempt on their part to make the contract bilateral so that they may be as free of India as India is free of them.

FRAGMENTS FROM A FOLDER

Wherever I am, the North-east is a place far away. There are certain areas in the world that are as distant as childhood, places that you can only dream about going to but can never quite reach. This is certainly true for the North-east: unreachable, unimportant, unknown. The distance between where I am and the seven states flung carelessly to one side of India is always the same — unbridgeable. In leaving childhood behind, we lose other things as well.

I carry a folder with me, a disparate collection of papers, maps, hastily jotted and barely decipherable notes, news articles, leaflets, an assortment of things that are summed up by a label that simply says "North-east." And sometimes, I like to think, this folder of mine is a fairly accurate symbol for the archival material, the government files, notations and plans, for all the news items and scraps of one-minute video footage that fill in the blank of the North-east for the mainstream Indian mind. Ten years after I began explaining to people that Shillong was in Meghalaya and not the capital of Assam, there is still an imaginary Indian border that stretches as far as Bengal — sometimes upto Assam — and stops there. For what lies beyond, there are those government files, a small body of books, the single-column news articles, all of which go under the collective rubric of the "North-east." Secession, then, for these North-eastern states is simply an act of ratification, a confirmation of their alien status, an attempt on their part to make the contract bilateral so that they may be as free of mainland India as India is free of them.

If this kind of distancing label is all that really characterises the North-east, how should one proceed? One could begin by reiterating the facts, running the statistics and the data past your eyes — and mine — in an attempt to flesh out this shadowy region for the unconcerned and supremely detached Indian mind. On a website put up by the North-eastern Council (one of the few sources of information on the web for a region where the total number of Internet users is less than that of any individual metropolis in the country), I tried to find some of these basic facts as a way of introducing you to the subject of my essay. And yes, the site tells us that the "region accounts for 7.8 per cent of the total land area of India." What seems more important to the NEC and the Government of India,

To the Indian government, the North-east is a liminal space, more outside than in — ninety per cent of its borders form India's international boundaries.

however, is its "strategic importance," the fact that nearly ninety per cent of its borders form India's international boundaries. More there than here, more outside than in, the North-east is the most liminal of spaces in this nation-state. Out of step with the future in its inability to join the nation in the race towards a "globalised" world, it is also cut adrift from the past, existing in a kind of timeless warp where it can only be considered under the formulae of problems and solutions. And yet what is the problem that we are trying to solve with regard to the North-east? On the NEC website, which stresses the possibilities for tourism and business in the North-east, there is not a word on the history of the region.

Not that I have something profound to offer. As I indicated at the beginning, this account has little authority. It depends heavily on a personal experience of growing up in Shillong and some intermittent interest in the region after I, for my own part, had been swallowed up by mainland India. But perhaps it is less insidious in being so deeply subjective, in its unabashed expression of the fact that this is no "portrait" of a region or of a people, but only a rearranging of the scraps that have gathered around the signpost of the "I."

To begin, then, from these memories is to look back at the newsroom of *The Statesman* in Calcutta, and to look at a photograph that had come in from the correspondent in Imphal, Manipur.

Perhaps the woman in the photograph had a name, but if she did, it has slipped from my mind. There was a caption that described the situation captured by the camera in a partially darkened room, but it left her unknown and elusive, the epithet "actress in a porn film" doing nothing to shed light on who she was and what the shape of her life might be beyond some definition as victim. The camera has caught the pallid complexion on her face as she sits in a chair, her knees together. You cannot tell the colour on the face of the two men flanking her, since their heads and faces are covered with scarves in an identical red-checked pattern. Their eyes seem to have no expression, and your attention is drawn to their powerful bodies and the automatic rifles in their hands. As for what the caption said, it was something like, "The... revolutionary group at a press conference today exhibited a former porn film actress...whom they had shot in the legs as a warning to the people to desist from such immoral activities. She was released and asked to lead a proper life."

It would be a wild exaggeration to say that this picture — briefly handled on a night shift at *The Statesman* newsroom — haunts me. What I can assert is that I have carried it along with other odds and ends in my head, as another inscrutable sign that demands an attempt at deciphering, as the reminder of one more life whose story needs to be told through one's imagination, if nothing else. Not that I will trouble you with fiction here. The present moment demands more prosaic facts.

The photograph was sent by *The Statesman's* correspondent in Imphal, a smart, educated Manipuri Meitei who had just been hired in an attempt to "increase the coverage" on the North-east. When I met him in Imphal a few years later, I brought up the photograph. It took him a little while to understand what I was referring to; after all, he had filed countless stories and photographs only to see most of them buried in the inside pages of the newspaper. But he soon remembered and ran the incident back for me, the press conference with the guerilla group that had exhibited the woman for the journalists. Didn't the punishment seem excessively harsh, I asked, considering that even from the perspective of the guerillas she must have appeared as an exploited individual rather than a part of the system they were fighting to overthrow? He reassured me that the woman had not been crippled, as I had thought, but that "the Party" merely inflicted surface injuries on her thighs as a warning to others.

To him, it was all part of the everyday world he had to negotiate. Sitting in an office with a sign saying that parcels and letters be deposited outside with the receptionist ("so that what happened to one of our colleagues in Kashmir doesn't happen to me," he had said, laughing), he could not have seen my curiosity as anything other than the passing interest of one more tourist with a typewriter, someone who would soon leave for Delhi or Calcutta and sink back into the inertia of the mainland. If one were to judge on the basis of the sporadic "special" stories that come out in the national media, it does seem that journalists visiting the North-east from the big cities are little more than tourists. This is not necessarily because they are unprofessional or unconcerned. It is because the mainstream media is very much a part of the government and the policies it occasionally chooses to criticise. In other words, the problem with the national media is that it is much too mainstream and conservative, concerned largely with the kind of stories that bring in the advertisers and keep the circulation going. A system which demands a quick turnover of stories has little time or news space for places and names that most Indians find difficult to pronounce. That is why most of the datelines in the North-east stories consist of state capitals, in spite of the fact that the percentage of rural population in the North-east is thirteen per cent higher than the national average.

Even the Kolkata papers, which are geographically closer to these far-flung frontiers than Delhi or Mumbai, find it difficult to focus on the North-east in any way other than a routine coverage of bandhs and encounters. When a story makes its way to the front page, it is usually because of the unwritten rule that says that the larger the number of people killed somewhere, the more important the news. For some of the reporters dispatched to the North-east to follow the trail of corpses, it is hardly worth their time and discomfort. I remember a photographer sent to cover the killings of a large number of Santhals in Assam telling me how he and the reporter had not even gone up to the relief camp. He was frustrated because it was much more difficult for him to get photographs without visiting the site of the story than for the reporter to get the details and to manufacture quotes, including, he had added in disgust, "fake sources, like a Brigadier who doesn't exist."

One cannot generalise from individual, perhaps apocryphal, instances like this. Nor can one say that stories are not manufactured with regard to other parts of the country. However, the absence of any kind of depth of coverage on the part of the media as a whole means that there is little compulsion to report accurately. Events in themselves are of little consequence, and the endemic weaknesses of the national media become that much more pronounced when one looks at the North-east.

The past ten years have seen a boom in the "local media" of the North-east, but the mushrooming of newspapers there has not meant better, more responsible journalism. Almost everyone I have spoken to in the region has characterised these new mastheads as instruments for channeling black money, more often than not an attempt on the part of the proprietors to leverage some power for themselves. Ironically, then, the growth of local media is not the expression of a functioning democratic system — as most apologists for liberal democracy would have us believe — but the symptom of a breakdown in civil society, where there are no safeguards for an individual or a people unless one is attached to some institution of power and can put a sticker on one's car that says "Press," "Army" or "Police."

To think of that photograph in this context is to feel the pointlessness of the situation, to see the act of violence contained in it as a somewhat desperate act. Apart from the fact that "the Party" in this case takes the easy step of "disciplining" an extremely vulnerable subject, the air of moral self-righteousness seems to be little more than a "reaction," in the political sense of the term. In warning the people through this act, the insurgents were expressing their feelings about the exploitation of the Manipuri people by alien capital and technology (the people behind the porn movies were said to be businessmen from outside the region), reacting to being subjugated by an alien culture that reduces them to commodities. But it is a culture so dominant that they must call a press conference to make their ideological point and stand before the cameras.

The first thing one noticed from the windows of the small Boeing drifting towards Imphal was the clouds. The plane kept remarkably low, so that the shifting landscape was visible between the thick pattern of the clouds, its vivid, rain-drenched green contrasting sharply with the hazy greyness that swirled below and all around us. Like most flights in the region, this one too was operated by Alliance, a poor cousin of Indian Airlines. There were three flights a week, the aircraft coming in from Kolkata to Silchar and then continuing on to Imphal. Sometimes, the flight did not make it from Kolkata; there were other occasions when it terminated its eastern journey in Silchar. But it was worthwhile trying to get a seat on this. It took half an hour by air as opposed to the ten hours on National Highway 53. And one could not be certain of reaching one's destination by road either, as I was to find out on my way back, when the bus gurgled to a halt before a broken bridge and we had to proceed partly on foot, and then in Marutis being operated by enterprising young Mizo men.

Even at first glimpse, Imphal was different from the prosperousness of Guwahati or Shillong, its half-built houses so different from the building boom evident in some of its sister capitals. I felt that I had travelled a little further away from India, and everything, the marketplace, the residential areas, the hotels and shops, confirmed this initial impression. One of the first things one notices on entering the North-east is the tattered, grimy nature of the currency in circulation. Small denomination notes that have been replaced by coins elsewhere in India are still doing their weary job here, torn and patched up, but still passed from rickshaw driver to passenger, from shopkeeper to buyer, as if everyone is going through the motions of an arcane ritual that no longer quite works. In Imphal, it was almost impossible to say that these scraps of paper were currency notes. People folded the pink two-rupee notes with utmost care, and it almost felt like a game, trying to spend the money before it disintegrated in your hands. To emphasise the condition of the money, moreover, was the cost of many basic things. Most goods manufactured in India are more expensive in the North-east, the prices going up in stages as one enters deeper into the region, but this process had come to a climax of sorts in Imphal. As some kind of compensation for this, there were things brought in from across the border with Burma (now Myanmar). As my last packet of Navy Cut ran out and I switched to smoking cheap WIN cigarettes made in China, Imphal felt very far from India.

The signs of underdevelopment, however, were not blatant. They were present but in a gentle, almost graceful, fashion that was very different from the startling contrasts visible in the plains of India. The rice fields surrounding the town were lush and green, the roads didn't appear particularly dirty, and people on the streets were neatly dressed. It took a while to register the things that were not quite right, like the unfinished houses with metal rods sticking out of roughly levelled roofs, the slow movement of goods and people in the markets, and the dull black scarves on the faces of the men hunched over their small rickshaws. Most goods were brought up to Imphal through the overworked and badly maintained National Highway 39, a 326-kilometre stretch of road that begins in Numaligarh in Assam and then passes through Nagaland to reach Imphal, terminating in Moreh on the

Indo-Myanmar border. This road, dubbed "Highway of Death" by journalists, is a popular subject for feature stories. It is not difficult to see why.

NH 39 is in a terrible condition, as was quite apparent from the tender notices in the newspapers for "Bituminous Road Works on NH 39-Manipur." The road is also divided between various Central and state security forces and different guerilla groups, all of whom extract their cut from the traffic on the road. On the Nagaland stretch, between Dimapur and Kohima, a minister's convoy had been ambushed, resulting in the death of his wife, daughter and grandson. In Imphal, the state government had "banned" the movement of MLAs and ministers — they were not supposed to go out without prior permission from the chief minister — and had asked them to be home before nightfall. Apart from this, there were frequent "blockades" and bandhs on the highway. A student leader from the All-Manipur Students' Union recalled how the road had been blocked by a Naga organisation after two Angami Nagas had been killed in a dispute. "We went and negotiated. Finally we came to an understanding. But it took a month."

At the time I was there, in April 1997, there had been a total halt in supplies to Imphal for twelve days because interstate truck operators had gone on strike, protesting against "frequent incidents of exortion." Fuel prices had gone through the roof, with petrol selling at Rs 45 a litre and cylinders of cooking gas at anything from Rs 400 to Rs 600 each. A couple of months after I left, *The Statesman* quoted a news agency report that announced the beginning of an "indefinite economic blockade" on NH 39 by the United Naga Council in protest against a move by the Manipur government to convert the Sadar Hills area into a separate revenue district.

That was one of the things I was to learn about Manipur, and relearn about the North-east, this complex mix of identities that rendered the situation far more ambiguous than a case of the state versus a disgruntled but united local population. At the time I was visiting Manipur, a series of tribal clashes had peaked in a cycle of retribution and counter-retribution, concentrated especially heavily in Churachandpur, a district below Imphal and bordering Myanmar. By the end of the year, official sources were claiming six hundred dead from these clashes alone, and over three thousand houses destroyed. The Naga-Kuki conflict had escalated steadily, but it could be traced not too far back to 1992, when territorial claims — especially control of the town of Moreh on the Indo-Myanmar border — found expression in armed battles. Informed observers in Manipur agreed that the Kukis had been armed by the Indian government at the beginning, to be used as a surrogate weapon against the Naga guerillas, but that they had rapidly become an independent force, extremely powerful in the smaller geographical area they controlled around the town of Moreh. Meanwhile, there was also some tension between the Meitei groups fighting for the sovereignty of Manipur and the Naga outfits fighting for a Greater Nagaland, primarily because tribal populations do not match state borders. For the greater part, the Manipuris and the Nagas have managed to contain these tensions, but they surface from time to time. The economic blockade by the United Naga Council may look strange to the outsider, since the Sadar Hills area is in Manipur, but there is a large Naga population there and it falls under the "Greater Nagaland" envisaged by Naga secessionists.

Beyond a cynical exploitation of the situation by intelligence agencies and a knee-jerk response to demands for new administrative units (whether they be full-fledged "states" or "autonomous district councils") these complexities are apparently not taken into account by the Indian government. And at a certain level, this is not surprising. The modern, secular nation-state adopted as a political model for India demands a certain flattening out of differences and the imposition of a structure that does not consider small or anomalous groups of people or nomadic movements. This is particularly visible with regard to tribal peoples, and as Ramachandra Guha has noted in his work on the British anthropologist Verrier Elwin, records of the All India Congress Committee at the Nehru Memorial Museum make barely any references to "tribals."

If nations have to be imagined into being, the people of the North-east may represent the most remarkable failure of that imagination with regard to India. At the same time, the responses of many tribal groups in the North-east, especially insurgency movements, may be seen as a reaction, an attempt to reconceive or re-imagine the model laid down for them by the nation-state they are ostensibly fighting. Without a larger entity of some kind such as the Naga or the Manipuri, how would they find a voice in the already crowded halls of the nation-state? If smaller tribes in this region have tended to group themselves into larger clusters, it is precisely to find

Insurgency movements in the North-east may be seen as an attempt by the tribal groups to reconceive the model laid down for them by the nation-state they are ostensibly fighting.

some form of leverage with the entity that is bearing down upon them. The ideal they are looking back to may be a more free-flowing way of life, but to resist something as monolithic as the Indian nation-state they have chosen to imagine their communities as sovereign political entitities which have never been subjugated. That is why their aspirations — in spite of frequent references to traditional village democracy — find expression in movements for nation-states of their own, whose boundaries, like that of all nation-states, are often blurred and bloody.

The various Naga tribes, distributed across Nagaland

and parts of Manipur and Myanmar, have cemented themselves into a larger entity to a great extent through the idea of a Christian religion they all have in common. In spite of this, tribal ideas of territory and local affiliation emerge from time to time. In the case of the Naga insurgents, this is exemplified by the two factions of the National Socialist Council of Nagaland (NSCN). One of the points frequently made by the group most dominant within Indian territory, the NSCN Isaac-Muivah, is that the Indian government should not try to include the NSCN Khaplang group in peace talks. Why? Because Khaplang is not a real Naga since he is a Myanmar Naga. The Meiteis in Manipur, too, are torn between different ideas of selfhood, caught between a desire to emphasise the Meitei culture that preceded the "Hinduisation" of the Imphal valley and at the same time aware that Manipur has its own strong version of Vaishnavite Hinduism. There are groups in Manipur which have objected vehemently to the Vishnupriyas in neighbouring Assam calling themselves Manipuri and although there are many arguments for and against, it ultimately depends on the idea that people who do not live within the boundaries of Manipur have no rights to call themselves Manipuri. I was to come across faces and voices again and again, sometimes in the course of a single day, that spoke of different levels of alienation. At the office of *The Statesman* correspondent one morning, there was a small man waiting to speak to him. He was introduced to me as a Naga village chief. Dressed in an old but neat western suit, he waited patiently for the correspondent to answer a couple of phone calls. Later, I was told that he had come for the correspondent's help because he could not visit the block development office

Security checks are routine in the North-east, and it is not uncommon to see the slightest gesture, cough, word being met by a sharp command and the deliberate swing of a gun barrel towards the offender.

to request some supplies his village needed desperately. "Why can't he go there?" I asked naively. He would be killed by the Kukis if he went there, I was told, because his village was in an area where the majority of settlements were Kuki, and the block development office was in the heart of the Kuki-dominated area.

A few days later, I visited Moreh, journeying the final segment of NH 39 before it ended at the border gates of Myanmar. There were frequent halts for security checks, soldiers in camouflage ordering us off and lining up the men on one side of the road. Some of them went through the belongings left in the bus while others searched the passengers. The slightest gesture, cough, word, was met by a sharp command — sometimes an outright abuse — and the deliberate swing of a gun barrel towards the offender. At one point, our bus had to wait at a checkpoint because they opened the gate only when there were enough vehicles to travel in a convoy. Most of the passengers got off the bus, gathering at the edge of the highway where the land sloped down in a rush of vegetation towards distant rice fields. A young Meitei in his early twenties stood next to me, occasionally throwing stones over the treetops. He pointed out the rice fields, glimmering golden in the early morning sunlight. "Burma, Golden Valley," he pointed out. I was about to ask him how far it was, but he let out a small sigh. Then he added moodily, "It was ours when Manipur was a kingdom, a rich kingdom. Nehru gave it away to Burma."

One final instance remains with me, a conversation that took place in Imphal as I took a rickshaw back from the market to my hotel. The driver remained low on his seat, his scarf tightly wrapped around his face in that defensive gesture of most rickshaw drivers in Imphal. But he kept turning back from time to time, stealing a glance at me. Finally he straightened up and slowed down a little. Moving his scarf down, he turned and spoke to me in halting Hindi. "Where are you from?"

"Delhi," I replied.
"You live there?"
"Yes," I replied.
"Have you seen the Jama Masjid in Delhi?"

When I told him I had, he asked me to describe it for him. It was uncanny, sitting in that slow rickshaw weaving its way through the by-lanes, past women whose graceful movements and faces and patterned long skirts could have belonged to Thailand or Myanmar, to be talking of the kites above the minarets of Jama Masjid and Karim's kebab shop in the alley across from the mosque. He sighed when I ran out of details. "Are you a Muslim?" I asked him. "Yes," he replied, and then went on, "There are very few of us here. It's a hard place to live in for a Muslim." Then he added as an afterthought, "There are many Muslims in Delhi, sir?" "Yes," I laughed, thinking of what the BJP would have to say to that.

When I got off at the entrance to the hotel, he didn't want to accept money. His parting words were that he hoped he would be able to visit the Jama Masjid some day. That was as far as he could go in his wildest dreams.

There is a curious scene in the opening pages of a book that tells of the victory of the Allied Forces over the Japanese in Myanmar. The time is July 1944, the place is Manipur.

> *These soldiers sitting in the dark at Manipur had come from Britain, India and Africa to fight the Japanese. They smoked; and they thought in a hundred languages. Some had driven trucks in Bermondsey, herded goats on the plains of India, and beaten drums after the reaping in Africa. All these men, white, brown, and black, had fought and endured in holes*

in the ground, had marched together and had spoken to each other in the bastard Lingua-Franca of soldiers from many countries.

The author, an officer in the 11th East African Division in the Fourteenth Army, feels a sense of pride in the enterprise that has brought these diverse men — Englishmen, Africans, Indians from the plains — together to face an invading enemy. I cannot share that pride, understandably, but I can marvel at the scale of European colonialism that succeeded in having Africans face off against the Japanese in the dense, tropical jungles of Asia. There are, presumably, no descendants of those Africans left in Manipur, but all over the North-east, there are people much like them: moved, displaced, and implanted ruthlessly to provide the cheap labour required for the great colonial enterprise. That is why, to even comprehend the North-east, one must begin by taking into account its recent history.

The descendants of those people who were moved around like chessmen are to be found everywhere in the North-east, in the Santhals and Biharis who constituted the backbone of tea plantation labour, in the East Bengalis who formed the small cogs of the British administrative machinery, in the Tamils who worked in the rubber plantations of Myanmar, and in the Nepalis and Gurkhas who served as foot-soldiers of the colonial government. To them one must add the successive waves of migration, some from the mainland of India, but mainly from what was first East Pakistan and then became Bangladesh, migrants driven by massacres, war, hunger, migrants who have populated the states of Assam and

Meghalaya and Tripura, creating demographic shifts and triggering violent backlashes. Every group derided by an epithet that was once popular in Assam — "Ali-Coolie-Bengali" (Muslims, Biharis, Bengalis) — came there as part of a process that was set in motion by colonialism.

Their presence does not make the North-east unique. It is a phenomenon comparable to many countries which have a sizeable Indian diaspora, such as Trinidad and Fiji, where after the withdrawal of the colonisers those who went as indentured labour find themselves at odds with the natives. It is also the kind of situation where one finds it difficult to take sides, because those who are exploiters in relation to the indigenous population are themselves people who have been exploited. The rage of the Bodos against the Santhals and the Bengalis in Assam is understandable, but it is nonetheless brutal.

I cannot claim to speak of these groups from an unbiased perspective, because my own past is intimately attached to them. As a child in Shillong, I discovered the absurdity of boundaries very early on, when I found myself being called a "Bangladeshi" by the local tribals and when I found the strongest of friendships breaking down under the weight of what seemed to be a distant past. To be an immigrant in the North-east is to be member of a group that fits nowhere, where some parts of one's identity always spill across the boundaries of classification. When I look back at that, I see myself searching for a place on the map, looking for a way to fix myself into the scheme of the nation-state, but also trying to find a spot in it that represents the place where I live. Neither history, geography, nor literature referred to the world we were growing up in; the All India Radio broadcast its distant events in a strange tongue that had no meaning for any of us, whether we were tribals or non-tribals. When, with the Asian Games in 1984, the first television sets made their way into our lives with their flickering blue screens, we found out about the world outside that stretched from Delhi to the United States, but we ourselves were somehow behind the screen, invisible. If we knew we existed at all for the world outside, it was because of a simple, empirical fact like Shillong and its surrounding areas being one of the wettest places on earth.

If, in spite of not really understanding why we were so ignored by the rest of India, so many of us moved away from the North-east and tried to become part of the mainstream that did not know of our existence, some of the reasons lay beyond us. For most middle-class immigrant children, the education and skills we were interested in acquiring meant that we would have to move away and stay away. Not only were there few jobs for us in the "undeveloped" North-east, but we were also outsiders and therefore, not welcome back.

Over the phone, across e-mails crisscrossing the globe, the conversations and thoughts inevitably turn to what was once home, about the place we all loved but cannot ever go back to, to the North-east as a place of perpetual loss and eternal love.

There are fashionable, and fascist, theories of nationhood that define the North-east as a problem on the basis of some shortcoming in the people who live there, a willingness

The hard truth is that the Indian security forces in the North-east exhibit every characteristic of an occupying army...and the effects of such power are bizarre.

to rebel being fostered by foreign powers, the Church, vested interests. Yet, if the hold of the state remains tenuous at best when it comes to the immigrant groups, it is a relation of outright antagonism with regard to those who have deeper roots in the region. The hard truth is that the Indian security forces exhibit every characteristic of an occupying army. In Manipur, at the heart of their military power is the Kangla Fort, a ceremonial Meitei site that now houses the Assam Rifles headquarters. From this, the security apparatus spreads out and infiltrates every pore of the landscape, the guns and dour faces a constant presence in everyday life. Army trucks with large machine guns mounted on them trundle down

NH 39, sunburned faces covered by black bandannas flying in the breeze. The checkposts vary in size but the routine of search and extortion hardly varies. Within the town, the army's presence seems less obtrusive but much firmer, and there were stories of the marketplace being cordoned off while the security forces conducted "combing operations."

At the time I was there, Manipur was under the Armed Forces (Special Powers) Act, a legislation that allows for military operation in areas declared "disturbed" and almost always leads to a virtual suspension of civil authority in favour of the military. Documents provided by the People's Union for Democratic Rights in Delhi indicate that this act originated as the Armed Forces (Assam and Manipur) Special Powers Act in 1958, and that some parts of Manipur have been under this Draconian act from 1958.

The effects of such power are bizarre, especially since there was something called the Army Development Group which was in charge of helping villages. As a result, one saw newspaper advertisements headlined "Gratitude," which consisted of the people of a certain village thanking an army officer, usually identified by name and regiment, for "distributing materials to the needy and poor villagers and for extending support for the development of the village." These expressions of gratitude existed cheek by jowl with reports of killings by unknown persons, of gunmen hijacking cars and of young men, usually in their twenties, being picked up by men claiming to be security personnel: "Family sources said no arrest memo was handed over by the uniformed men, who came in a white Maruti Gypsy, no. HR 23A/1600."

One day, walking past the headquarters of the Manipur

FRAGMENTS FROM A FOLDER

Rifles (the armed wing of the Manipur Police), 1st Battalion, I stopped to watch the young tribal recruits climbing down from their trucks. Automatic rifles slung over their shoulders, they exhibited a sense of power and purposefulness as they spread out in front of their headquarters, but the most striking fact about them was what they had done with their uniforms, or in spite of them. The camouflage or battle-green trousers were hanging fashionably low from their waists, some of the boys had Ray-Bans on, while almost everyone sported some form of headgear, either colourful bandannas or baseball caps with the peaks pointing backward. It was charming and youthful, but those guns were real and it was a reminder of their counterparts — perhaps their brothers and sisters — in the jungles. In Assam, the peace process ran aground when the surrendered ULFA cadres turned out to be a greater nuisance than the actual insurgents, robbing and plundering with impunity, under the benevolent gaze of the Congress chief minister Hiteshwar Saikia. Government policies do not take into account what happens when all you teach an entire generation of young people is how to handle a gun, whether overtly in the service of the state or indirectly by forcing them to revolt. But everywhere in the world, the disbanding of armed rebels has rarely been followed by genuine peace. In Latin America, they call it "post-guerre" — after the little war — when rebels become members of violent gangs, because structurally nothing has changed.

It is difficult to see how the Indian government will resolve such situations. With a literacy rate of sixty per cent, Manipur had the highest percentage of educated unemployed in the North-east when I visited it. The rickshaw drivers in

Imphal who keep their faces hidden by scarves do so because they are educated, some of them even graduates, and they are ashamed and do not wish to be recognised. One afternoon, I was given a ride by a Meitei engineer who was unemployed. "There are no vacancies, so I applied for a driver's position with the state government," he said, laughing, as the bike flew along the dirt track he had veered into. "The minister called me at home and said I was too qualified for the job. He did not listen when I said I would rather be a driver than sit around doing nothing." We had moved away from the marketplace and the central area of the town. The houses were more infrequent now, scattered unevenly around the scrub land. In the distance, there were the barbed wires of an army garrison, but the engineer turned into another little dirt road to take a shortcut. There were no gardens, no lawns attached to the houses we passed, silent in the afternoon, but as we rode deeper into the zone, the memorials to the martyrs killed by the Indian army began to appear, uneven concrete shapes like broken fingers pointing at the sun.

That was a long time ago, but recently I visited the websites of some of the guerilla groups. There was a feeling of déjà vu when I saw pictures of the memorials, and the North-east seemed both near and yet far away.

War In A Time Warp

■ Ajit Kumar Jha

In Bihar's Jehanabad district, landless labourers have challenged the might of the landlords, leading to an economic blockade, a breakdown in social relations, and gang-based killings by both sides. The story of a land stuck in a time warp.

WAR IN A TIME WARP

PIPRA, Jehanabad: Once it was sheer hunger that compelled Sant Lal Sapera, alias Rangeela, to risk his life everyday. Waking up at dawn, he would search for, lure and trap all kinds of venomous snakes with his bare hands, simply by imitating their hiss. Today, there is an entirely different reason for his daily dalliance with death. This snake charmer of Pipra village, in Jehanabad district, no longer removes the poisonous fangs of these deadly creatures. He leaves them there in the hope that the snakes will protect him and his community from the marauding mercenaries of the Ranvir Sena, the private army of upper-caste landowners in this central Bihar district.

Rangeela uses soft chants to train the serpents to attack. The chants, which he calls "Shiva mantras" (prayers for Lord Shiva), may appear simple, but actually they are like the kiss of death. The snakes, no matter where they are hiding, always respond to his chants. They are at his beck and call as if he is the pied piper of the venomous pits.

UMTA, Jehanabad: The entire hamlet of Umta sleeps by day but stays awake the whole night, with the male adults, armed with rifles, keeping a vigil on rooftops. There are eight rifles in the double-storey house of Laxmi Nandan Sharma, an upper-caste Bhumihar landlord whose family owns three hundred acres of land. The house looks like a fortress, its iron gates padlocked even in the middle of the day. The Sharma household is terrified of Naxalites, the radical militant guerillas, who have been organising the landless labourers in

The upper-caste landlords of Umta in Jehanabad are so terrified of Naxalites that they keep their gates padlocked even in the middle of the day.

the area. In the summer of 1998, in nearby Senari village, sixty-six Bhumihar landowners were slaughtered by the Maoist Communist Centre (MCC), the most radical wing of the guerillas.

Sharmaji's nephew, Kedar Nandan Singh, was murdered in 1985, when Naxalites allegedly broke into the house searching for rifles. The landlords and the police then retaliated by unleashing a reign of terror on the poor farm labourers residing in Pipra and its neighbouring villages. The labourers, in turn, boycotted farm work. They also announced an economic blockade against the landowners but their demand for higher wages remains unfulfilled till today.

After a while the blockade became unsustainable. The workers, having lost their means of livelihood, suffered more than the landlords. Some of them wanted to come back but the landowners decided to teach them a lesson by refusing to take them back. Today, most of the labourers have either migrated to nearby towns for work, or taken to different occupations available in the area, or simply end up starving. The landowners have either switched to tractors and the use of modern machinery to reduce the dependence on manual work or simply let the land lie fallow. Today, most of the Sharmas' three hundred acres lie uncultivated.

Its name derived etymologically from the calm and serene Buddhist *viharas*, Bihar has, ironically, degenerated into a modern metaphor for barbaric violence and fierce lawlessness. Massacres, inflicted in the dark of the night by a dominant caste on a subordinate caste, have become a regular phenomena. Often, these are accompanied by the burning down and looting of villages and gangrapes of defenceless Dalit women — acts of vengeance intended to heap humiliation on the victims. Equally brazen and as grotesque are the retaliations by the Dalits.

The gangbang style of violence, however, started in Bihar only in the mid-Seventies — it was a reaction to a new kind of confrontation. A new challenge, from below, in the form of the Naxalite movement, to the traditional inequality and hierarchy built into the rural land and social structure. The Dalit hunting, in turn, is a reaction by brutal upper- and intermediate-caste landowners, otherwise at loggerheads with each other, to the radicalisation of the landless labourers by various Maoist outfits.

Periodic hecatombs are, however, confined mainly to central Bihar. Its Magahi- and Bhojpuri-speaking areas are marked by a machismo culture. Carved out of the old Gaya district, ironically the site where Gautam Buddha attained moksha some two millenia ago, the district of Jehanabad is notorious for the highest number of gang-based killings in Bihar. Starting from the Parasbigha carnage of 1980, in which dozens of Dalits and backward caste farm labourers were slaughtered, there have been scores of massacres in the last two decades leading to the killings of thousands.

While in Laxman-Bathe village on the banks of the Sone river, close to seventy-five Dalits were gunned down by the Ranvir Sena, in Senari, as retaliation, sixty-six Bhumihar landowners were slaughtered by the MCC. Both these carnages were committed in Jehanabad. Over a dozen such ding-dong battles have taken place in the district in the last two years.

Prima facie, there is conflict between the upper castes and the nouveau riche "backward caste" Yadav and Kurmi landowners, yet in places the latter support the Ranvir Sena. In fact, politicians from across the political spectrum provide both overt and covert support to the Ranvir Sena. For instance, King Mahendra, the notorious Bhumihar landlord who made his millions in the spurious pharmaceutical trade and who introduced carnage-style violence in Jehanabad, won the 1980

Lok Sabha elections as a Congressman. Today, he is a Rajya Sabha MP from the Laloo Yadav-led Rashtriya Janata Dal (RJD). The reason: even conflictual caste identities merge when the confrontation is class based. Even backward caste political parties like the RJD and Samata have now become parties of the new landlords — the Yadavs and the Kurmis. There is little representation in these parties of Dalits and of extremely backward castes like the *saperas*.

These subordinate groups of landless labourers have at times organised under the banner of the Lal Sena, an armed outfit of the various Maoist organisations. Dr Vinayan, a follower of Jai Prakash Narayan, founded the Mazdoor Kisan Sangram Samiti, a mass-based Naxalite organisation. A protracted and brutal class warfare prevails among these two broad categories of the landowners and the landless.

The hamlet of Pipra (named after an old banyan tree), in Jehanabad district, has about 125 houses. These belong mainly to Dalit and backward caste labourers who have lost their farm jobs in the economic blockade between this hamlet and the landlords of Umta. When I visited the village on a sultry July afternoon in 1999, the villagers were busy entertaining themselves by watching Rangeela, the snake charmer, playfully provoke his cobras and *karaits*, *dhamans* and *ajgars*. There was gaiety and laughter in the atmosphere. Humour has kept the poor alive. Joviality and conviviality is the life blood of this community.

In order to escape the torrid heat inside the badly-ventilated, but cemented, one-room tenements, about a hundred people were assembled in a *marwah* (open-air platform with a canopy). The houses have been built under the Indira Awas Yojana — the Central scheme of housing for those under the official poverty line.

Rangeela is the most well-travelled member of the community of Pipra. In search of these slithering creatures, he has gone as far as Assam, to the dense forests of Kaziranga. He has even ventured into the dense Manipuri jungles in

Rangeela, a sapera *in Pipra village in Jehanabad, is a backward among backwards — his caste is so low in the pecking order he does not even get the benefits accorded to Dalits.*

search of *kala nags*. Looking after a family of eight, at fifty-eight, this magician of the dense forests continues to court death to eke out a living for himself and for his community.

Since *saperas* are not considered scheduled caste, Rangeela does not possess a pucca house under the Central government's poverty alleviation programme. He also misses out on the patronage doled out by the local RJD government, which claims to benefit "backward castes" (BCs). While most of the goodies are cornered by the Yadavs and Kurmis, the privileged creamy layer among the BCs, the *saperas*, low down in the "backward hierarchy," and lacking a political voice, clearly end up as losers. In a forward looking futuristic world of "social justice," it is his unfortunate fate to remain backward.

Only two of Rangeela's four daughters are married, the other two are "burdens" on his stooping shoulders. His three sons — all of whom have lost their jobs in the economic blockade — are no props in the autumn of his life. "I need to marry off two of my daughters... I cannot continue to feed them with the few rupees per day that I make," laments Rangeela.

The friendliest face of all in Pipra is that of thirty-year-old Surendra Paswan. He, however, hides tremendous worries behind that charming smile. Burdened with the pressures of bringing up two children and five nephews and nieces, he has worked as a *bataidar* (a sharecropper) since his teenage years. He used to work for Babu Revati Raman Singh (brother of Kedar Nandan Singh).

Since the days of the blockade Surendra has been forced to migrate to Mumbai, where he works for a cloth manufacturing company for Rs 1,200 a month. He hardly saves a paisa, and is heavily indebted to the local moneylender, who squeezes something close to a thousand per cent annual interest on the principal amount. Yet, Surendra is happier these days since he does not have to face the occasional blows of the landowner's sons. His womenfolk are also safe at home and not vulnerable to exploitation as in the past. He has a pucca house.

Ganesh Das, fifty-five, however, does not share the happiness of Surendra. "We are *kamiyas* (bonded labourers), sahib, we have a pucca house, but an empty stomach." Blockade or no blockade, more than half the people of Pipra still go to work in Umta village in Singh Sahib's house, explains Ganesh. "The blockade is an excuse. I am ready to work for three-and-a-half kilograms of rice and one-tenth portion of the produce, but I never get work for more than six months in a year," Ganesh points out.

"Every time there is a murder in Jehanabad, the police come and beat us. We work in their homes the whole day and, in return, they call us Naxalite *ugrabadi* (Communist extremists). Where do we have the time for Naxalite activities?" Ganesh is almost on the verge of tears. His twelve-year-old child, Harendra, is suffering from polio but he cannot afford the cure.

The *nakebandi* (blockade) lasted for one entire year after the murder of Kedar Nandan Singh. "You should have seen the reprisals. They thrashed every male member of this village blue and black, and even molested some of our women. They did not even spare the children and the old folks. So many of us were arrested and several of our villagers are still in jail. Not a single member of this village had any idea who had murdered the old man. Apparently, some people had property differences with the Sharma family and they had hired musclemen to kill the old man," Rajnikant Paswan, a young man of twenty-eight, points out.

"We work ten to twelve hours a day, for which we still get three kilograms of rice, including *nashta* and *khana* (breakfast and lunch). We never get any clothes and certainly no work for half the year. The blockade is maintained by the *maliks*, not the *mazdoors*," Rajnikant argues forcefully.

"Life is as rotten as it used to be. The only saving grace is the three kilograms of rice for an entire day's work. This has provided some relief in an otherwise extremely difficult life," Surendra Paswan says, agreeing with the other two.

The village has no piped water, two to three *chapa kals* (handpumps for water), out of which one or two are permanently out of order. In fact, most people suffered from *hughuggi* (amoebiac dysentery) since they drank water from the nearby tanks and rivers. Most women have four to five children and have lost an equal number in childbirth. Literacy is close to nil. In fact, the only student who had passed high school and entered a local college was Anil Kumar, twenty-one, who spent most of his time taking the old and feeble to the nearest dispensary in Maqdoompur town.

"We have a *bam dal* of twenty to twenty-two adult villagers who keep vigil at night from 7 pm to 3 am. They have torches and lathis. All we do is shout if we hear any shooting in the neighbourhood. Sometimes a constable comes from the local *thana*. He has become more regular after the Miapur massacre of Dalits and backwards in Aurangabad in 1999. The tension is tremendous since the Senari killings where sixty-six upper-caste men (mostly Bhumihars) were killed by the MCC activists," Rajnikant explains.

"How do you protect your womenfolk?" I ask the men.

"Our men cannot afford to protect us. We are not as fortunate as our *malkins*. We need to work to feed our families. Therefore, we learn to protect ourselves," Sunitia Paswan, a thirty-two-year-old mother of four, who had been patiently listening to our conversation from a distance, butts in.

Poverty, ironically, breaks the backbone of patriarchy, I find myself thinking as we drive ahead. It is quite clear that the whole district is torn apart, both economically and socially. Parents of prospective brides in Patna, the rumour went, would never get their daughters married to boys in Jehanabad, lest they get widowed right after the marriage. In fact, in some cases in the past, wedding parties were targeted during large-scale killings. The backwards see every young Bhumihar in the area as a potential member of the Ranvir Sena, while the upper castes see every Dalit as a Naxalite.

The red porous sandy soil, on both flanks of the Patna-Gaya road, appears to be covered with a velvety verdant carpet as the summer heat gives way to the monsoon. Although there are no puddles of muddy water, the wetness of the soil is evidence of the downpours that had taken place the previous day. Miles and miles of light green, freshly germinating paddy seedlings, and a darker shade of taller wheat plants and baby maize cobs, are interspersed with heavily laden mango groves. An agreeable aroma of unripe mangoes, mixed with that of newly dampened soil, hangs in the air. The late summer laziness is gradually fading out. There are signs of activity all over. Peasant women in colourful muddy sarees are at work with a sickle and a wicker basket, cutting grass for fodder or getting ready for an early transplant.

The different hues of lush green patches gradually thin out. The mango orchards appear somewhat barren as I approach the twin towns of Jehanabad and Maqdoompur, after a two-hour drive from the capital city of Patna. A certain pungency replaces the pleasant fragrance in the air. The reason is not hard to fathom. Even as dark smoke billows from the low chimneys of the hundreds of brick kilns lined up on both sides of the road, heavy grey dust emerges from the few stone chip crushers that also make a peculiar grinding noise. Huge billboards announcing the wonders of Lafarge cement appear here and there, as if announcing a local boom in the construction industry.

I remember the puzzle that struck me the first time I crossed Jehanabad on my way to Bodh Gaya: With countless brick and stone chip units, how come Jehanabad does not have a single well-constructed house? Despite the intricate architecture of the ancient Hindu temples and the magnificence of the monumental Buddhist monasteries in the vicinity, the basic elements of the art of construction do not seem to have even occurred to the modern civil engineers of the town. Ditto with lanes, bylanes and the drainage system. The whole town is one big mess of puddles, craters and garbage.

The local administration's attempt to widen the roads, by

pulling down the encroachments on both sides, has failed in its basic purpose. While the front of the buildings appear as if bombed out of shape, there are mounds and mounds of rubble heaped on both sides, making the streets even narrower than they were to begin with. This causes tremendous traffic jams with rickshaws, bicycles and bullock carts competing with overloaded trucks, buses and other four-wheelers. It also gives an appalling appearance to the entire area. Maqdoompur, a smaller town, is in some ways a replica of Jehanabad, at least in terms of its shoddiness.

I am glad to leave the stench and sights of the twin towns behind. Just outside the city's limits, the well-constructed highway, excellently maintained by the Japanese for the benefit of international Buddhist tourists going to Bodh Gaya, provides a great comfort. The return of the verdant environment at least for a few miles comes as succour. However, as clumps of dry grass and cracked earth start replacing the leafy surroundings, I begin wondering whether we are once more approaching another shantytown. The local guide announces it is Umta hamlet.

Tension is palpable almost everywhere in Umta although my visit does not coincide with any massacre. Turbaned men, their faces covered with scarves, whiz on Bullet motorbikes, while the women invariably have their faces partially covered with a *ghunghat*.

I wonder if we have reached a large village since all the green patches have disappeared. We stop to ask a passer-by on a bicycle. "No, not really, there are only about a hundred families in the entire village. *Ish elake mein Nakebandhi hai sahib. Ishi karan sare khet parti pare huen hain*" (There is an economic blockade in the area, therefore all the fields lie fallow).

We make a right turn in the direction of the village and drive for a while. It is fallow land on both sides of the dirt track, despite the fact that a river, locally called Morhar, runs right beside the village. A few buffaloes, their tails flicking flies, are grazing in the vacant fields. We suddenly find ourselves entering the driveway of the largest *kothi* in the area, a two-storey poorly built redbrick building, which has the appearance of an abandoned fortress. The entire front yard and the front portion of the house is encircled by iron stakes and collapsible iron gates.

Since there is neither any sentry at the door nor a doorbell, we simply resort to crude honking. Two men in dhotis, with the sacred thread hanging loosely around their shoulders, emerge rather reluctantly after about ten minutes. There is someone in a shirt and pyjamas behind them with a gun. My profuse apologies somehow reassure them and they invite us in for *chai* and *gur*. As I approach the front grills, from the corner of my right eye I notice the silhouette of a woman peering out from behind dark drapes. She is standing behind one of the corner windows of the top storey. Although curious, I quickly look away. No one notices. The three men accompany us to the front porch and provide us with a string charpoy and a couple of plastic chairs to sit on. After the initial chitchat, the two men in dhotis begin talking.

One of them is seventy-year-old Laxmi Nandan Sharma, the Bhumihar landlord, whose three hundred acres of land

115

Seventy-year-old Laxmi Nandan Sharma, a landlord of Umta, calls the Naxalites "ungrateful" and says the government is "spoiling" them.

have remained largely uncultivated for several years. He explains that the economic blockade declared by the Dalit labourers has gone on in Umta, and the nearby hamlets, since 1985.

"What is the reason?" I ask.

"Why else, simply because of rumours and canards spread by the Mazdoor and Kisan Sangram Samiti (MKSS). They call themselves Party Unity these days. They are simply murderous Naxalites," Sharmaji says of the Dalit activists of the area.

"What sort of rumours?" I ask.

"That our family confiscated three hundred acres of *gairmajarua* (government) land," Sharmaji explains rather excitedly.

"Did you?" I deliberately keep my questions short and innocent.

"Are you crazy? We owned these lands, and much more, for generations," Sharmaji asserts.

"Then why did the villagers — I mean the farm workers — get convinced by the Naxalites' rumours?" I ask.

"Let me explain," chips in forty-year-old Ramanuj Sharma, Sharmaji's grandnephew, who has been listening attentively to us. "The Naxalites taught our farm servants to double their wage demand without doubling their work load."

The farm workers had been demanding three kilograms of grain (about Rs 30; the official minimum wage is roughly Rs 35 for eight hours of work) and one-eighth share of the produce even before the murder. Earlier they used to take one-and-a-half kilograms of grain and one-tenth share of the produce. "But instead of extending work from ten hours to twelve hours, they demanded reduction of the work day to just six hours. This was outrageous," adds Ramanuj indignantly.

"Therefore, we chucked the workers out for sometime hoping that they would ultimately relent. But they remained stubborn with their demands. They began boycotting our fields. We let them stay uncultivated for two years. Meanwhile, the administration, i.e., the local sub-divisional officer (SDO), intervened. He agreed to their demand of three kilograms of grain, and suggested one-tenth of the produce. But even when we agreed to the SDO's suggestions, the labourers simply refused to turn up for work," elaborates Ramanuj.

"When ghee doesn't come out with the help of a straight finger, then we try a crooked finger, don't we," Ramanuj says by way of justifying the use of the Ranvir Sena. Of late, the Sharma family had been taking covert help from the Ranvir Sena, who were reportedly stationed across the local Morhar river, to pressurise the former workers of Pipra to return to work on old wages, and their womenfolk for domestic chores.

"Imagine their cheek, they began saying that they would turn up only when they had *phursat* (free-time). While they did have *phursat* for others' work, they did not for us. Is this fair?" old Sharmaji joined the conversation once more.

"But after all, they are not bonded labourers. Don't you agree it is for them to decide who they should work for?" I ask.

"No, technically speaking, they are not *bandhua mazdoor* (bonded labourers). But imagine — one of them said, '*kam na ho to, hartal ho to*' (We'll quit work, we'll go on a strike). This is what we get for giving them a job, providing them land for houses and taking care of them whenever they are in need," Sharmaji laments.

"What happened to them after you threw them out of their houses? Even if they worked for others, where did they manage to live?" I enquire.

"This is precisely where the entire problem began. They all got pucca houses under the Indira Awas Yojana. Most of these *mazdoors* ended up with their own houses. I remember twenty of them got it initially. Later the *sarkar* got so lenient that one of them, who had four sons, ended up with four houses. Imagine the luck of these *mazdoors*, each got a house for himself under Indira Awas Yojana scheme and all this reward for no work. Our *sarkar*, in fact, is their *sarkar*, it is simply spoiling them," Sharmaji adds regretfully.

The *sarkar*, of course, refers to the government of Laloo Yadav and Rabri Devi. During his first term, Laloo Yadav used the Central funds to build some houses for the Dalits under the poverty line.

"Do these *mazdoors* belong to any particular community?" I ask to change the subject.

"All of them are Chamars, you know, cobblers. They call themselves Ravidas, the government calls them scheduled caste and the Naxalites call them comrade Dalits," Sharmaji says sarcastically. Ramanuj provides exact figures of the labourers' population: thirty to thirty-five houses of Ravidas, ten to twelve houses of Nonia and Kahar caste, thirteen to fourteen houses of Pasi and some other labourers from the neighbouring Pipra village — essentially all scheduled castes.

"Once the boycott and the blockade began in full swing, we switched to tractors. We ourselves began ploughing our fields. They responded by lighting fires to our fields of *chana* and *masur ka dal*. They burnt the entire crop and the administration simply kept mum. In fact, the SDO charged us that we had started the fire ourselves. How ridiculous! But as I told you, it is their *sarkar*," Sharmaji adds in a sarcastic tone.

"They were still not pacified. In fact, they next came and looted one of our rifles. When my father objected, they shot him. Father died ten days later. We simply could not do anything despite our frustrations. They were the ones who instigated violence, totally unprovoked," Ramanuj adds in a choking tone.

"What was your late father's name?" I ask.

"Kedar Nandan Singh. He was a patriarch, a very religious man who believed in peace and nonviolence," says Ramanuj.

"What did you do to counter the violence?" I ask.

"Oh we believe in nonviolence. It is the influence of Buddhism on us. We simply informed the police and they carried out some arrests. We got back our rifle."

"If you believe in nonviolence, why do you keep rifles?"

"Well, mainly for protection. After dark, we shut the entire house. All the iron gates and grills are padlocked. All of us men go up to the roof with all our guns and ammunition. We stay awake and alert, way past midnight. We sometimes simply fire in the air, at other times shout something to keep others awake. Hearing us the local police turns up to patrol the area," Ramanuj explains.

"Do you have enough arms and ammunition to protect yourselves?" I ask hesitatingly, not sure if it was the right question to ask.

To my surprise, pat comes the reply: "Don't worry. We have seven guns and one rifle — all licensed," Ramanuj reveals. "God has sent protection for us recently in the form of the Ranvir Sena. It has been quite active on the west side of the Morhar river giving sleepless nights to the Naxalites and their country cousins."

"What about your enemies? What kind of arms do they possess?" I venture boldly.

"They have *kattas*, I mean *desi* (countrymade) guns, all unlicensed. That is why they came to rob us of our guns and rifles and in the process killed my father," Ramanuj said, maintaining a cocksure certainty.

"Hasn't the decade-long economic blockade practically

ruined your family? What other source of income do you have?"

"Yes and no," old Sharmaji interjects hesitatingly. Ramanuj explains that since they cannot attend to the crops at night, instead of paddy and wheat, they now grow *chana* (grams), *masur* (lentils) and *matar* (peas). Besides, paddy requires enormous labour, especially during transplantation.

"We had sixteen bullocks in the past, we have only one now. We have also replaced our stock of twenty cows with two tractors, which we drive ourselves," Sharmaji adds.

"Were there any eyewitnesses to the murder," I suddenly find myself asking.

"Yes, my mother," for the first time the guy with the gun speaks. He is Madhav Achari, a sub-inspector with the Indo-Tibetan Border Force. My thoughts veered back to the woman at the window.

"Can I speak to her?" I ask.

"Yes, you can, but not to the other younger women of the house who live upstairs," Sharmaji pronounces firmly.

I was escorted upstairs by Madhav to a balcony overlooking the fields and there I met his mother, the fifty-eight-year-old Chinta Devi.

"Were you looking out of the window when I arrived?" I ask.

"No, it was one of my *bahus*. Neither they nor I are ever allowed to venture out of the house, so we peep out once in a while. In fact, since the murder took place, we do not even

For upper-caste women like Chinta Devi, always in purdah, the new insecurity has turned the house into a prison — they are not allowed to step out of the house anymore.

step down to the lower floor where the men live," she complains.

Patriarchy created the purdah system for women here long back. But the recent conflict in the village, the atmosphere of violence, has made it virtually a prison for the women. The economic blockade has further made the landladies into housemaids with a shortage of domestic help.

"Do you recall any violent incidents before the murder?"

"Yes, there was a dacoity, the year after my wedding. The dacoits took away everything — jewellery, utensils, clothes, cash — nothing was left. But they did not kill or hurt anyone. No one was arrested. Years later, after the children were born, there was a fire in the haystack. Almost the entire house burnt down. Yet no one was hurt.

"The dacoity by the Naxals was shocking. They came at the dead of the night, some ten to fifteen young boys, most of them without even a moustache. There were no men in the house except for my old father-in-law who was busy reading his *Ramayana* downstairs. We were only women and children — all of us equally terrified. They came up straight and asked for the rifle. We had no clue where it was. But they knew its exact whereabouts as if they had been informed by an insider. They broke the almirah, took the rifle and some twenty thousand in cash and left. While returning, when my father-in-law questioned them as to why they were creating a commotion, they turned around and shot him point blank. They saw that he did not die, but yet they left. Clearly the intention was to create confusion so that no one would chase them," she narrates the entire account in one breath, as if offloading herself for the first time.

"Other than restricting your movements, how has the blockade affected you?" I ask.

"We no longer have any *dai-nawri* (domestic help). We have to deal with all the household chores ourselves. At one time, whole families of maids used to live with us. They would simply work the whole day for one kilogram of rice. We would occasionally give them some clothes during festivals. Today, there is no one even to eat our leftovers," Chinta Devi laments.

Perhaps that is one positive result of the decade-long standoff in Jehanabad — the Dalits are no longer willing to eat their former masters' leftovers. Yet, among the landlords, a fierce feudal streak is still left over from their glory days, and they obstinately cling to it, resisting any kind of change.

LULL AFTER THE STORM

■ MEENAL BAGHEL

> If Orissa's supercyclone washed away lives, its aftermath snuffed out dignity for those who survived. The story of the cyclone and how little has changed in the state since then.

LULL AFTER THE STORM

The family pauses before the coiled silver snake in the compound of Bhubaneswar's Lingaraj Temple. The father, a small-built man, oiled hair slicked back, wearing ill-fitting trousers, holds on tightly to his two identically dressed boys. They are not twins, but not too far apart in age either. All three stare at the intricately carved icon before moving on. Trailing behind, the mother, a young woman in a bright yellow polyester saree, hesitates. She takes out a fifty paise coin from her change purse and puts it in the thali overflowing with offerings of all denominations. Some more hesitation before she retrieves fifteen paise from the platter: a five and a ten paise coin. With her thirty-five paise offering, she then seeks a final and frantic benediction.

They have come from Bartak village, where her husband works, or rather worked, in a school. "He would ring the bell to signal recess and end of class," she elaborates. When the waters came in, the school collapsed as did their partly-pucca home. Their buffalo, tethered to a pillar, was swept away as the column crashed. They have no money now. *"Kuch paise nahin hain."* She stresses *"kuucchh."* But they took a small loan from an aunt in Cuttack to go on a pilgrimage. After Lingaraj, it's Lord Jaggannath's turn next. "All four of us are alive. Could I ask for a bigger miracle?" she wants to know.

On the morning of 26 October 1999, walking the short distance from his home to office, situated on the periphery of the Biju Patnaik Airport, D.C. Gupta, director of the Bhubaneswar meteorological office, marvelled at the pleasant weather. In the office, however, his attention was caught by the whorls and the sharp movement of the graph on the monitoring unit. "A cyclonic storm of low pressure area from the Andaman Sea and adjoining areas was building up." But such a build-up at this time of the year was not untoward and Gupta was not overly concerned.

Thirty-eight hours later, on the evening of 27 October, he received an urgent call from his office. The angry whorls on the monitoring unit had become opaque. It was almost certain that they were in for a "severe cyclonic storm." Gupta decided to issue a storm warning though still hoping that the pressure would divert towards Andhra Pradesh or West Bengal and soon dissipate as had happened often in the past. By next evening, buffeted from the lashing wind and rain, the director and his staff monitored in stunned silence the onset of the supercyclone. (Among other things, cyclones are categorised on the basis of wind-speed. For instance, the wind-speed during an average cyclone is 60 kmph, 185 kmph during a very severe cyclone and if it touches 240 kmph, meteorologists categorise it as a supercyclone. In the supercyclone that devastated the eastern coast of Orissa, the average wind-speed was 260 kmph.)

The rains that began from 11.30 pm on 28 October, continued without relent for the next forty-eight hours and the wind impelled the ferocious sea nearly thirty kilometres inland. For almost thirty-six hours, tidal waves as high as twenty feet swatted the coast. Over ten thousand people died, almost all poor, nineteen lakh trees were uprooted and about fifty thousand homes destroyed.

In Bhubaneswar, the BBC crew was readying to leave when I landed. International spotlight, always restless, had already moved. Perhaps to Chad, Somalia, Sarajevo....

Over ten thousand people died and about fifty thousand homes destroyed as the cyclone lashed the eastern coast of Orissa.

In the city, sleepy hotels and alert taxi-owners clung to the sharply revised tariffs to cash in on the unexpected bounty of journalists and white foreign aid workers, and in Ersama block of Jagatsinghpur district — in the lush paddy fields and the serene Hansua river — there were still bodies bobbing around, clumps of flesh, barely together.

Driving across the 480-kilometre-long eastern coast, the landscape narrated its own story of trauma: thousands of coconut trees bent in precisely choreographed movement, acres of paddy in rigor mortis, ancient banyan trees collapsed, their roots exposed like a jungle of wires in a gaping electric box. On the main road near Rahama village, six poles doubled up in a line as if in a tug of war with an unseen adversary, a bus with its top blown away, girders of an unfinished construction caught genuflecting to a higher force. The entire countryside seemed frozen in a moment of flight. Those who survived, simply sat outside their broken mud dwellings, talking in hushed tones, their eyes registering only the comings and goings of journalists, strangers, officials, NGO workers.

If there was silence in the countryside, there was chaos at the office of Special Relief Commissioner D.N. Padhi. The babble of instructions, the jangling of phones, the thump of files, the scraping of chairs, the sound of confusion. The body count was pegged at ten thousand but the enumerators had yet to travel to the villages of Jhatipari, Kankan, Padampur....

The army, which was brought in to restore law and order after the food riots broke out, had stayed on. For Operation Sahayata: To help build roads, ferry the scavengers to the still flooded areas, set up food camps, and in the midst of complete haplessness, to signal a sense of purpose.

Captain Mann of 8 Engineers' Regiment from Agra offered a ride in the shallow, almost flat-bottomed BAUT (an acronym for Boat Assault Universal Type), which was also carrying a group of Anand Margis from Bangalore who were helping with the scavenging. At Jhatipari village, still submerged, they leapt out like Allied Forces did at Normandy in World War II and waded through marshy banks and paddy fields to retrieve bodies.

LULL AFTER THE STORM

The rat-a-tat-tat chug of the army boat brought a few villagers onto the banks. The sound usually signalled food, water, tarpaulin...rationed hope. But when they saw the Anand Margis they turned away: more bodies. Of kith and kin, but mostly of strangers. Retreating into a corner they stonily watched the Anand Margis sprinkle boric powder on stagnant water, fish out corpses, often two at a time, pour kerosene on them and cremate.

Across the villages in the Ersama block, which accounted for eight-and-a-half thousand deaths — on main roads, in the interiors, in the paddy fields there were piles of ash which scattered away bit by bit each time a vehicle thundered past or when the evening breeze gathered pace. A quarter of a soul here, an ounce there.

Now the living wanted nothing to do with the bodies.

"They sometimes even eat sitting next to a corpse," said Captain Mann. Both he and Acharya Karmadhisanand Avdhoot, who looked more like an athletic beach bum than the leader of the scavengers, impressed upon the villagers the importance of disposing of bodies. "Otherwise there will be more disease. More death," said Captain Mann to his unheeding audience. But picking up a rotting, faceless blob of flesh was obviously not easy. It also meant acknowledging another death. More loss. "I cremated nine members of my family. I will not cremate even one more body," said a gaunt-looking villager at Jhatipari mutinously.

Standing next to a makeshift hut, put together with four bamboo spikes and his wife's saree, and the carcass of a buffalo, Sapan Rahane spoke about the loss of his family: fourteen members. Among them his daughter and young sister. When the waters started to rise and the thatched roof of their house flew away like a wayward kite, Sapan perched both the girls on his shoulders and swam towards a tree. "For nearly eight hours, through the dark, the rain and the howling wind we sat on that tree," he pointed to a half-submerged stump. "Suddenly, the gale picked up.... I was wet and tired and could not hold on tight as my little girl was snatched by the wind and fell into the swirling waters below. I saw her go." The gale also forced him off the tree. "Fortunately I got wedged between two thick branches but in this struggle my sister too slipped away," he said.

Sapan stopped looking for them some days after the cyclone. There were others to cremate and the living to look after, including his eighty-three-year-old father who hadn't eaten for two days when we met him. He lay shrivelled, spent and hopeless inside the hut. The corpses and the carcasses, said Sapan, had become a part of life, just another hardship, among the many others, to overlook.

On the way back to Bhubaneswar that evening, the road was clogged with traffic. Hundreds of trucks with number plates that testify to the vastness of this country had lined up patiently to disgorge the relief material that had come pouring in from all over. Clothes from Andhra Pradesh, foodgrains from Punjab, sweaters, drinking water, utensils, more clothes from Jammu and even two fire engines from Mumbai! And then there were the sightseers from Cuttack and Bhubaneswar who came in carloads to "see" the ravages of the cyclone. They

LULL AFTER THE STORM

came with packets of biscuits and bread which they threw from partially rolled-down windows of their moving vehicles at the villagers lined up on the roadside.

Outside the Kalinga stadium in Bhubaneswar there were yet more trucks carrying relief material. But there were no takers — most of those affected were still stranded in their villages. Except for two exhausted gatekeepers at the stadium, there was no official system to channelise all these goods to those who needed them. At the state secretariat, in a shabby anteroom painted in that bilious shade of blue so favoured by offices of governance, there was an animated discussion on about the photograph of chief minister Giridhar Gamang that

Relief material could not be distributed for a long time as there was no official system in place to channelise the goods to those who needed them.

accompanied the government's appeals in all newspapers. "*Yaar*, how can anyone take our appeals seriously with the chief minister looking like this," said a bureaucrat. "On the contrary, this is meant to rouse sympathy. If the chief minister looks so hapless, just think of the rest of the population," sniggered another amidst much jollity. Over endless slurps of *chai* and sympathy for the poor, the conversation veered towards allegations made by the vice president of the state BJP unit, Shayamanand Mahapatra, about corruption in the procurement of polythene sheets and blankets. Thirty thousand superior quality blankets sent by the United States as part of the aid package were overnight airlifted to Calcutta by a prominent businessman and allegedly sold there after the labels were removed. The consignment was then replaced with coarse, inferior blankets (eventually only ten per cent of those affected by the cyclone received blankets).

News of these scams had yet to reach the affected people who were in any case busy scrounging around for food. In the priorities of survival, blankets and polythene were way down on the list. For the moment. "Not a single grain of the relief rice has reached us. For four days our children have not eaten anything. Tell me, if you can reach here, why can't the government?" demanded Narayan Mahapatra at Hosnabad in Badchana block.

More than the headlines and the words, crammed, struggling to breathe in the confines of newspaper column inches devoted to news of the cyclone, it was a photograph that caught one's attention and pinned it: A horde of men rushing towards the camera. Some, hands outstretched, others, teeth gritted, running under the shadow of a plane taking off. From

LULL AFTER THE STORM

the grainy columns of bad newsprint their faces leapt out, grim, desperate, pleading.... "Hungry villagers chasing an Indian Air Force plane dropping relief material," read the caption. Within days followed news of attack on a helicopter carrying defence minister George Fernandes, Biju Janata Dal (BJD) chief Naveen Patnaik and Congressman Jual Oram by famished villagers and food riots breaking across the state. "Oh! but all that looting came to nothing," snorted Narayan Mahapatra. "You see, people didn't know where to keep the loot as the homes of most were still submerged!"

Less than a hundred kilometres away in the compound of the block office at Ersama, there was no place to walk, stashed as it was with sacks that had come in from all over the country. Even as I wandered around looking for someone responsible to talk to, more consignments were being unloaded. "Hey! You madam, come up here, we will chat," motioned a man perched on the roof-top. Treading across a mountain of sacks of wheat, rice, maize — food, nourishment, sustenance, life — I introduced myself to Digamber Mohanty. "IAS on special duty for this block," he pronounced. He had been parked at Ersama for the last one week, as had been all the food. So why was it not being distributed?

"We have to first make a list of all that has come in and from which part of the country, then make another list of who gets how much, and tally it with the voters' list. As you know all the roads have been washed away. How can we cart all these to the villages? We also have to chalk out a food for work scheme (under the scheme, villagers who helped in the rebuilding for a stipulated number of hours were to be paid with food). I don't have enough manpower. I myself haven't slept or shaved for four days. My family also needs me back in Bhubaneswar...." Then, in the same breath, almost as a non sequitur, Mohanty added that Operation Nirmal (a programme to desalinate the wells) that had recently been launched had been "quite successful." "So far, we have successfully disinfected 525 wells under the scheme," he elaborated with evident satisfaction.

It was tempting to mock Mohanty but for the fact that he was at least there. Sleepless and unshaven, as he pointed out, but in the field, struggling to accomplish a job for which he had never been prepared. He was unlike many of the district collectors who, daunted by the enormity of what confronted them, had fled their homes and responsibilities as the cyclone broke out. The chief secretary of the state, who was in the US with his ailing daughter, did not return till well after a fortnight. Chief minister Giridhar Gamang was, for the better part, in Delhi on a multipurpose mission: to demand "Rs 10,000 crore" as the aid package from the Centre; to joust for one-upmanship with George Fernandes, who headed a task force appointed rather belatedly on 13 November, a full fortnight after the cyclone; and to persuade Sonia Gandhi not to remove him. At the village and block levels there were other reports of abuse of authority. While desperate villagers scrounged for food and drank from stagnant pools of putrid water still carrying carcasses, in Balikuda and Jagatsinghpur districts, the police arrested block development officers, a chairman of a panchayat and ten other junior officials for

LULL AFTER THE STORM

siphoning off large quantities of relief material: rice, pulses, polythene, blankets, biscuits and even packets of bleaching powder.

As greed pitted against need, the line between the law-enforcer and the law breaker was washed away.

The absence of administrative control was conspicuous across the devastated land. From Puri to Paradip, it was the NGOs, the Anand Margis, the RSS workers, and individual volunteers who travelled through nonexistent roads and crossed broken bridges, injecting glucose and a sense of purpose into a dazed people. During a trip to Ambiki and Jirielo villages, two young boys halted our car. One of them was bent double, vomitting his guts out. They wanted a ride out to any stretch that resembled a road. Both Narendran Sides and Hemsagar Patel were nineteen and members of the Nagar Sena in Bilaspur in Madhya Pradesh. They came to Orissa to help after watching reports on the cyclone on television. "But when we came here we realised that everything is chaotic and there was no one to tell us what to do," said Patel. The only thing that was most obvious to them, and also the most difficult, was to dispose of the rotting bodies. "They were all over the place and obviously needed to be cremated."

Equipped with sticks, cloth, kerosene and their humanity, the two friends moved from village to village. Earlier in the morning, they had found a group of six people who had tied themselves around a coconut tree to avoid being swept away. "But I think the tree crashed on them. We found their corpses, still chained to the tree," said Patel. His friend took this rather badly. Exhaustion, stress, discomfort, and death at its most crass, had taken a toll on the boys. Patel spoke of wanting to go back home while the still-green-faced Sides quietly looked out of the car.

Like Patel and Sides there were others. Men and women who find their justification, their adrenaline, their cause in troubled spots across the globe. The Nobel-winning Medicine Sans Frontier, World Vision, Red Cross, Centre For Youth and Social Development (CYSD), Lutheran World Service, Bharat Gyan Bharati, Utkal Bipanna Sahayata Samiti had all set up rehabilitation camps, and organised food, shelter and first aid.

At one such camp, set up in a now defunct school at Mallipur, I meet Rabindra Rout, 39, "intermediate fail" and an itinerant minstrel. He walked from Paradip to Mallipur after his house was washed away. Rout was warm, garrulous and something of a jester in that makeshift court. After sundown, as the night sank in, he sang to the gallery in his ripe, raspy voice. Entertaining villagers, sad, broken men and women who had little to go back to. His ouvre ran from Oriya folk songs to *Mera Jeevan Kora Kagaz* and *Dil To Pagal Hai*. A little over a week after his arrival at the camp, Rout had gone off tangent in the middle of one of these sessions and launched into a verse about the cyclone. "It was as if he went into a trance," said Shivnarain, one of the volunteers at the camp. Since that evening Rout's behaviour had been marked as rather erratic. He often moved around muttering about *baarish*, *paani*. Shivnarain said that he was exhibiting classic symptoms of post-traumatic stress disorder.

Through Ersama block and Bhadrak and Astarang

districts, there were others as traumatised as Rout. At Nokkipur village, teenager Dulla Rani Bhol, with her eyes screwed tightly shut and her hands clasped around her head, refused to move from her crouched position in the corridor of her pucca house. Two days before I met her, Dulla Rani, who had been abandoned by her husband, lost her newborn child. "During and after the cyclone we didn't get food for several days. Her milk also dried up so she couldn't feed the child, who then died," her mother explained. The girl had since gone into shock.

At Cuttack general hospital, overflowing with limp, listless patients, we came across a woman who had turned mute after

A cholera patient being taken to a health centre. With one doctor for 64,178 people, Orissa has the lowest number of doctors per capita in India.

battling the waters for two nights and two days. She had wandered in alone and the doctors were administering her first aid but didn't know what else to do with her. With barely enough doctors to treat people for dehydration, cholera, cuts and wounds, there was clearly little hope of treatment for those suffering from post-traumatic stress disorder. (With one government doctor for 64,178 people, Orissa has the lowest number of doctors per capita.) "Probably they will end up being branded mad," said Satya Misra, who was documenting cases of post-traumatic stress syndrome for a Bhubaneswar-based NGO.

It was Satya who told me about the lone survivor at Sonadia. "I have heard that she is sixty years old and the only one alive in her village which has been completely swept off," he said. "The village is just here, would you like to come?"

The "here" stretched to eternity. Under an overhead sun we walked for about six kilometres guided by the stale stench of death — possibly the bleached animal carcasses. There was not a living creature in sight. Our guide, Sunil Mondal, from the other side of the Sonadia village, came to a halt on a bare tract of land, barren and sandy. "This is it," he said, looking around. "This" was also where 150 families had lived before the cyclone.

The woman we had come looking for was not there. And there was no way of finding out where she could be.

Instead, like excavators, we discovered shards of pottery, a pack of scattered playing cards, a bicycle, its axle twisted beyond redemption, a lantern half-filled with water, the same that swept away its owners, an aluminium school satchel with a corroded pencil box, a tattered quilt tangled in the bushes, a saree etched in the white sand. Spools of tape from an audio cassette, which children from a neighbouring village had skilfully strung up on a tree, gently swayed in the breeze to some unheard music. This was the low lying side of Sonadia village where the Harijans lived as also the immigrants from Bangladesh, men and women who travelled inland via Midnapore, and who don't account as the dead because in the state rolls they never existed.

On a raised mound a coconut tree caught the eye. Four framed photographs dangled precariously from the scales of its bark: that of Lakshmi, Ganesh, another one depicting the nine planets as deities — Shukr, Shani, Budh, Mangal.... Overlapping them was a school photograph, a class of children posing with their teacher. The same man appeared in the fourth photograph taken obviously with the other teachers of the school. All of them belonged to Hemant Karan, a math teacher at a middle-level school in Japa.

On one corner of the mound was a heap of gutted ribs and soot. "The policemen burnt the bodies of 'Sir' and eight members of his family here," said Mondal.

No one will know what happened to "Sir", his family, his neighbours on that dark night. Did they face heart-pounding fear or was death instantaneous? Did they scream? For the moment, there was only calm and the barest whisper of the wind.

Across the 480-kilometre-long coast of Orissa, several villages or chunks of villages, as in Sonadia, had been washed away. Existing now as only specks in a map, altering forever the demography and the psyche of a land. At Dhobei, a few kilometres from Sonadia, the only graduate of the village, 35-year-old Khirahatti, had been killed. "He was a wise man. He taught us many things," said his father-in-law Dharendu Pradhan. He also saved his village. On the evening of the twenty-eighth, as Khirahatti was returning from the neighbouring village, he heard the cyclone warning on the radio. He ran back all the way and exhorted the villagers to shift to the *bedi* (literally, higher ground) across. "He kept telling us that the water would surround us soon and helped evacuate fifty families," recalled Pradhan. The waters came in as Khirahatti and his seven-year-old son went back to fetch their belongings. Three days later the villagers found the bodies of the father and the son clasped to each other. At what must have been Khirahatti's house, we just found a skull, no one was sure whose, and remains of an educated life: a green book, its stiffened pages curled like wavelets. While most of it was in Oriya, the back of the book section was in English: A collection of poems. *Friends* by Miss Asha Mohanty, *Literacy And Family Welfare* by Miss Pushpa Mohanty. The introductory poem was by Mister Srikant K. Sarangi, Ist year (Eng.Lit.), titled *Love And Death*:

"Death is so quick and Life is so very shorts (sic) and fragile/ why waste your brief spans of life in anger and hatred and violence? Love and love always to defeat death that lurks near the corner."

Apart from the aged father-in-law, there was Khirahatti's young widow. No one was sure what would become of her.

She wasn't the only one. "Virtually every family in the

area has been fragmented leaving thousands widowed or without parents," said Jagdanand, the chief coordinator of Centre for Youth and Social Development (CYSD), a cash-rich Bhubaneswar-based NGO. Caught up in the exigencies of providing immediate material relief, neither these agencies and certainly not the government, seemed to have any long-term plans for them. Travelling around we saw many young boys with shaven heads and girls sitting forlornly, or swinging listlessly from fallen trees. The only time they perked up was when they saw a car or a relief truck. Peering through the glass of the car, they would ask for a "*biskoot*."

But while the children were at least temporarily being taken care of by the neighbours, widows, especially the younger women, were much worse off. Those who had returned to their parents' houses were not given their quota of government relief: two hundred grams of rice, forty grams of dal, ten grams of salt per day, as they had been delisted from the area's voters' list after marriage. And at a time when every grain of food was precious, these daughters, though beloved, were still a burden.

Many of the widows who stayed with in-laws were forced to go and beg on the main roads. At Bodeilo in Ersama block, we were told of a twenty-two-year-old widow who had committed suicide after being allegedly forced to beg.

If the cyclone washed away lives, its aftermath had snuffed out dignity.

Three months later, as the state went in for assembly polls, to elect a fresh set of people to govern them, I revisited the villages that had been battered by the cyclone.

The speck on the map of coastal Orissa dissolved into a sylvan village as we reached Mallipura. Patches of brilliant neon-green paddy, low clouds, and nearby, an oval lake bordered with bottle green algae. Lithe, bare-bodied charcoal brown men out of a Nandlal Bose painting standing around, aimlessly, as if installed to complement the landscape.

Then, there were also the trees, their spines broken, houses, with roofs caved in, roads, ruined beyond repair, and the silence of complete inactivity. In the distance, the whisper of the wind mingled with the sound of children chanting: Vote for BJD, Vote for BJD. Democracy had reached where the administration couldn't even months after the devastation.

Further down, at Ersama, at Sonadia, at Dhobbai, it was a similar story. Half-alive villages, ruins intact, watched bemused as jeeploads of men, men on sturdy motorbikes, on cycles, sailed past, throwing pamphlets, exhorting them to vote for their candidates. Two days later, roughly 1.29 crore voters, thousands of whom had lost their all in the cyclone, were to exercise their franchise.

This right had come at a price. The little that was being done by way of relief work had been stopped to honour the election code of conduct. Many *tehsildars* in charge of assessing damage and compensation were preoccupied with election duty and nongovernmental agencies had been asked to stop distributing relief material till polling was complete.

At Dhobbai, which had lost sixty men to the cyclone and which now survived on a dole of APL (Above Poverty Line) rice — twenty kilograms per month, per family at four rupees a kilo — poll preoccupation meant a delay in the delivery of that rice. But if they didn't get bread, they at least got tamasha.

So, Tohali Prasad Das, who organises labour at Paradip, laughed when he heard that BJP star Vinod Khanna had addressed a rally at Bolgarh in Begunia assembly constituency, promising "development" work if the BJP-BJD candidate was elected. "These leaders," Das paused for effect. "They always say, 'We will turn the soil into gold'," and his appreciative audience erupted into raucous laughter.

Despite an abundance of bauxite, coal, marine life and tourist attractions, Orissa firmly remains at the bottom half of the country's development index. Something like the Peru described by nineteenth century naturalist Antonio Raimondi: A beggar sitting on a bench of gold.

Successive governments have honed indifference into an official attitude. And clues to their sins of omission are all over, for anyone interested in finding out. The proposal for setting up warning radars on coastal roads and embankments, mooted in December 1999, is still at proposal stage. Three months on, there were only twenty-three cyclone shelters across the state. Effectively this meant that if there was another cyclone warning, the state was no better prepared to deal with it. Mangrove forests were cleared to facilitate shrimp farming, which has been banned by a Supreme Court order, leaving the coast without a buffer against cyclone waves. Poorly constructed schools under the ambitiously termed Operation Blackboard collapse like straw houses in a cyclone, much needed polythene is misappropriated, food production, according to a recent economic survey, has steadily declined and in Dhobbai, seventy-year-old Diwakar Lanka says he had not seen the condition of his village better in his lifetime.

But there is change. During conversation young men casually use words like exit polls ("learned from the radio"). Ghanshyam, a matriculate and a farmer, at that time jobless because he had lost his implements in the cyclone, spoke about the need for "politicians to respect the people and not the other way around."

Diwakar Lanka's son Ajay Kumar tried to explain what democracy meant to him. "It means election first and then," he slipped from Oriya to English, "personal sovereignty." Ajay completed his post graduation in political science from Utkal University. He returned to the village after he failed to find a job. He wanted to educate children in his and neighbouring villages but found that he couldn't be a teacher without a B.Ed. "Now I don't have the money to study further," he said. Ravindra Swain, another jobless farmer, handsome in a blue pinstripe Louis Phillipe shirt ("came with the relief material"), rebuked quietly when asked who he would vote for. "Isn't that personal?"

At Ersama, standing outside the local Congress office, Chaya Sahu, grandson perched on her hips, clapped as she watched workers embark on a rally. Sahu came to Ersama after her house in Arada village was washed away. Does she support the Congress? "No." So why does she clap? "I clap for all leaders, all rallies. Since I have two hands I might as well clap," she philosophised before trundling away with her grandson.

"You can no longer take the electorate for granted," says Naveen Patnaik, who has stepped into the rather large shoes of his father Biju Babu. Part-time writer, part-time socialite/ dilettante, friend of Jacqueline Kennedy when she was alive and now a full-time politician, Patnaik is the man who eventually swept the hustings.

Touring with him as he crisscrossed the cyclone-ravaged coastal belt days before the polls, was an insight into electoral politics. Up in the air on the chartered Mesco helicopter, he preferred grim silence. But as the big bird readied to descend at a venue, he would wave and smile and just before the final leap onto the ground, arrange his hair in a nervous, reflexive way. His speech at all the meetings was succinct, similar. Greetings in Oriya for the new year, expression of hope for a new century before quickly lapsing into Anglicised and rather brutalised Hindi. A cursory mention of the cyclone, the trauma that the poor have undergone, a dig at J.B. Patnaik, his rival in the Congress, and the final charm offensive, in Oriya, of course: "I am here to serve you, to serve, to serve you."

Thunderous applause.

Of course, there is a postscript to this. Patnaik's exhortations to his people to love him *tikke-tikke* (literally translated, little little) were rewarded with a landslide win.

In the year since the cyclone there were other Orissa stories in the headlines: Dara Singh, the white tigers at Nandankana, drought. And there was a trickle of cyclone anniversary stories. Two caught my eye: One was about how only 112 of the 750 Members of Parliament have delivered on their promise to give Rs 10 lakh from their

MP's fund for relief work in Orissa. (Of these there are only three from Orissa.)

The other one, datelined Bhubaneswar, 18 September 2000, is quoted verbatim from *The Indian Express*:

An organisation called the Centre for Legal Aid to Poor had organised a public hearing yesterday at the Soochna Bhavan here for the victims of the supercyclone. The victims came from different parts of the state to voice their agony and their grievances against inefficient rehabilitation efforts in the past ten months.

However, if the "prosecuting" side of the hall was jam-packed, the "defendants" were all missing. Neither Chief Minister Naveen Patnaik, nor any of his cabinet colleagues and bureaucrats who had been invited bothered to attend.

The cyclone victims were visibly disappointed. But given a platform to speak they poured forth on the irregularities in the rehabilitation and reconstruction work launched by the state and the "inhuman treatment" meted to them....

Standing in the "dock", 80-year-old Usharani Nayak of Jajpur could not hold back her tears as she recalled the morning of 30 October 1999 when her entire family was washed away. Now, "even ten months after the assurances, I am living in the verandah of the block office," she said.

Maid In India

■ Vijay Jung Thapa

> The maidservant is an invisible Indian right inside our homes. This story brings out the utter loneliness of one such maid in Delhi, who works sixteen hours a day for a monthly salary of Rs 2,000.

Funny how a single word can stir up such emotions. Shanta, as usual, was sitting in the corner of the large carpeted living room of the Mehra family, watching TV, in the hour just before her chores for serving dinner would begin. The Mehra family was watching the 9 pm news — not very seriously though, and even Shanta, sitting quietly in her place, was more bothered about how the *mushroom matar* that she had cooked would be received on the dinner table. That's just about when she heard the news presenter say the word, "Pankhabari," loud and clear. She didn't really pick up the rest of the news item, which was about an assassination attempt on a prominent Gorkha leader in Pankhabari. No, all she remembers is that her mind blanked out everything else except the name of her home town. "Right there, right then, I had a vision of my house back home and I realised how homesick I was. You know, I came to Delhi because I just had to get away from that place. Now, as I grow older, I think about going back all the time." For the next few minutes or so, Shanta remembers sobbing quietly in her corner. Nobody in the Mehra family noticed, nobody even remembered she came from Pankhabari. After the news, she shuffled out quietly to lay the table and serve dinner. And later, nobody said a word about the *mushroom matar* either.

Shanta is thirty-seven years old, a native of the Darjeeling hill areas, who has lived in Delhi for the past thirteen years. Out of these, she has spent the last seven years with the Mehra household. She is muscular in build, has a pleasant round face with dimpled cheeks and a beauty mole just above her left upper lip. The Mehras — more or less — find her to be a conscientious worker, honest and clean, though they do admit that she occasionally slips into one of "her moods" that leaves her wandering from room to room in a hand-wringing daze of depression. But Shanta says she enjoys working for the Mehras — because they are more considerate than all her previous employers. She has a routine, she says, and she sticks to it. "If I do my work properly, they let me be. I can't ask for more."

The routine, though, is relentless. And it adds up to almost sixteen hours of work in a day (excluding a two-hour break in the afternoon), all for a salary of Rs 2,000 a month. It involves her getting up at five in the morning. The first thing she does in her little three-by-three feet room, tucked away above the garage at the end of the driveway, is start warming water in her little electric heater. She is particular about hygiene — and likes to bathe before she faces her gods (a collage of calendar prints in one corner of her room) and use the tiny bathroom before her neighbour, Ram Naresh, the household driver, can get a chance. "I wasn't really religious… but I grew up in a family where religion was like an addiction," she tells you. Of all the images of home that flash in the mind's eye, the one that remains pristinely clear is that of her attending the regular evening prayers with her family. Her father, a hardworking daily wager, who heaved two-hundred pound loads onto trucks for a living, was a deeply religious man who made sure the entire family congregated for evening prayers. Shanta, her father's favourite, was always the one who got to hold the *diya* in one hand and a bell in the other as the rest of them sang in praise of god. "When the images of those days come back to me, I'm always wearing white and I have flowers in my hair. I sing in the highest tone and my father sits passively looking at me dotingly, silently mouthing the words."

Her morning ablutions over, Shanta shuffles down the steps in the early morning darkness and enters the Mehra household from a side door, for which she has a key. The door opens into the kitchen — and straightaway she dives into her work: fixing cups of tea and coffee, readying for breakfast and packed lunches for the household. About half-an-hour later, there is a click on the door that connects the kitchen to the rest of the house. It's Mr Mehra, who gets up early for his morning walk — and is usually the first one to give Shanta access to the rest of the house ("You have to be careful these days with hired help."). He helps himself to his usual cup of filter coffee, tucks the morning papers (which Shanta has brought in) underarm and heads for the balcony to enjoy his beverage before he sets off for a brisk walk that's been prescribed by the doctor. Shanta usually smiles behind his back — she likes Mr Mehra and she knows his secrets. For instance, very often, he doesn't go for his walk. He hangs around, reading the newspapers, lounging in an easy wicker chair—and when somebody else awakens and comes out to join him, he pretends he's just come back after three strenuous rounds of the colony.

" I like him, you know...he's gentle, he's nice. I've never seen him lose his temper," she says of Mr Mehra. She seriously believes it's a class thing — affluence and comfort ushers in dignity and sophistication. "You are a nice and gentle person, because you have lived a life of luxury," she tells you. She has formed this theory because she keeps comparing Mr Mehra with her late husband. And almost always, this kind of comparing leads her back to dark rooms of the past where the walls seem lined with razor blades. "Jeevan (she has no qualms naming him) was a violent man. He was always drinking the local liquor or rolling dice. And if he still had time he was running around with bad women...but somewhere in that messed up brain of his, he still loved me." Her eyes brim up. "What do you know about Darjeeling?" she asks. "Nothing much except it's a pretty place and good for a holiday, right?" But she has a different story to tell about those back-alley dirt roads of her home where life could be full and rich, but also harsh, hard and mean as a snake. Men like Jeevan (and it seemed like a whole generation of them) led a hard life with little or no education ("even with education all you can become is a teacher"), looking for work in tea plantations, or lifting loads up in the city. And when they did make some money, it was squandered away quickly in drunken binges inside seedy thatched-roof bars — that threw you out on the street when you were dead drunk. Next morning, if you weren't already dead, you got back to work. It was hard. It was as if God made them pay for the loveliness of their scenery by demanding everything else. Jeevan died three years into their marriage (he was thirty, she twenty-four) — they found him outside on a street, his insides pickled with liquor, an empty bottle propped up between his legs.

"More toast," shouts Mrs Mehra from the dining table, jolting Shanta out of her reverie. Once Mr Mehra and the three Mehra children leave home for work, a warm tranquillity seems to descend on the house. Shanta sits in the kitchen, savouring the moment, perched on a small wooden stool, sipping her cup of tea. But soon Mrs Mehra comes calling — a thin bespectacled lady who has a hawk eye and is very house proud. Right after breakfast, Shanta is up to her elbows in work — dusting, swabbing and sweeping the various nooks and crannies of the large three-bedroom house. This takes a good two hours — after which it's straight into loading clothes into the washing machine and cleaning the three bathrooms of the house. Then, it's off to the kitchen to cook lunch. Shanta doesn't enjoy cooking so much, in fact when she joined, there already was a cook in the Mehra household. However, with time, the cook left for a better job and since an alternative couldn't be found easily, she was eased into cooking too, though the Mehras did hike her salary by Rs 500. "I've complained quite often that I have too much work — look at this house, isn't it big? I do everything here," she says. But all she gets to date are assurances: "We're looking. It isn't easy to get good help these days."

Post lunch spells a two-hour break for Shanta. She remembers a time when she used to look forward to this. A time when she would go out to the nearby public park and mingle with the hired help from the other houses in the neighbourhood. They would exchange stories about their employers ("I can tell you things about every house in this colony"), joke, talk about upcoming holidays, who's romancing who and then head back when the sun's rays started lighting up the rooftops of the colony's houses. "But one day I got into a fight with some of them...especially those who come from Bihar." She rolls her eyes. "I can't stand them. They make up things about me. Just because I don't entertain them and I'm single." She says she has relatives in Delhi — "It's such a big city, it attracts everybody. I have three cousins and an uncle living in different parts here." But she rarely goes out to meet them — for two reasons. One, she's terrified of traffic and never ventures out alone — "I can't handle all these buses and trucks. I don't know the roads." And second, she is ashamed to meet them. Ashamed to be a woman with rough, callused hands, ashamed to be wearing donated clothes, ashamed that she wears old, frayed shoes with the toes worn clean through. "They (the relatives) are from my mother's side, all educated and doing well. I know it's false pride…but still I just can't seem to go out and meet them."

So, in the end, what Shanta ends up doing nowadays during her afternoon break is shutting herself in her room. Inside, there is a myriad of choices on how to spend the afternoon. There, on a side table, lies a worn-out radio that seems to continuously belt out Hindi movie songs. These she loves. Not the new ones, but the older ones, those with melody and feeling. She seems happiest, sitting in her bed, the afternoon sun highlighting her hair, with songs from the Sixties or Seventies coming through the airwaves. "Now that's a song," she says happily after a particular number, "Did you know I was seven years old when that movie came out." Often, she thinks hard about going home ("maybe this Dussehra") — she hasn't for the last five years, but then gets worked up because she really can't think of anybody who would be happy to see her. "My parents are dead and my brothers are all drunkards," she says. "One of them is dead. I didn't hear anything about him for years until a yellow postcard came along telling me he'd died six months ago." Often too, she falls asleep lying in her bed, leading to Mrs Mehra ringing the bell (attached inside her flat), summoning her in for tea. Then, she scurries down the steps and into the kitchen, apologising shrilly. By this time, one or two of the children are back — and she gets busy making tea and sandwiches (usually cucumber or tomato, with the crusts cut off). Later, as she clears the teacups and side plates, she looks inquiringly at Mrs Mehra, who starts dictating (amid much prompting from everybody) what dinner will consist of.

Shanta hates it when people come visiting — like tonight. "It's not the extra work, but the fuss," she points out. Mrs Mehra though likes to keep repeating how Shanta suddenly becomes sullen when told that there were going to be guests. The Mehras like entertaining, and every other day there are guests for dinner. Usually, at least from Shanta's viewpoint, these dinners are nothing but a big show. Mrs Mehra usually "inspects" her attire, often asking her to change into a smarter looking saree: "Whatever happened to that new saree I gave you last year." She's supposed to be smart, courteous, alert and yet invisible — and that point is not entirely missed by Shanta. "If I'm there (out in the living room serving guests) for even a minute more than necessary, I can see the tension in memsahib's eyes," says Shanta. She remembers how once she was admonished for inquiring from a guest (who lived in the neighbourhood) how her maid was doing. But she's reconciled to this, and works quietly in the kitchen, going out only when summoned. "When guests come home I'm like a cross between a circus horse and a donkey. Out in the living room I'm the horse — looking good, preening, smiling and serving the public. Inside the kitchen, I'm a donkey — slaving away, cooking, cleaning and washing," she says laughing. "But I don't mind. This is my work," she adds.

Late at night, much after all the guests have left, and the Mehra family is fast asleep, Shanta locks the side door to the kitchen and winds her weary path up to her room. There isn't much left to do now except kneel before her calendar gods for a few minutes more. There, in the stillness of the night, she prays for everybody she knows or can remember at that moment. "I pray for Jeevan, I pray even for all my brothers," she says. "But most of all I pray for the safety of the Mehra family because in the end they are all that I have."

'DO RATS HAVE RIGHTS?'

■ RANDHIR KHARE

> From deep inside tribal territory in Madhya Pradesh and Maharashtra, a rare portrait of a marginalised and misunderstood people forced to live as scavengers. An impassioned plea for us to first understand the tribals before thrusting development plans on them.

'DO RATS HAVE RIGHTS?'

I

I have had a long and personal attachment to the district of Jhabua in Madhya Pradesh. It had begun, of course, with an official assignment in 1985 and continued "unofficially"...not with activist groups and development agencies or any political or social work groups...but just with people. And the attachment to a people and a region is like an enduring emotional relationship. One becomes acutely aware of every change and shift.

Except that in Jhabua, apart from the surface spit and polish, nothing seems to change.

In 1998, I had advised an international health agency to consider assisting communities in Jhabua. They appeared very keen. So I enthusiastically contacted the "relevant authorities" in Bhopal. They asked, "Why Jhabua? The district is full up with international, national and local NGO assistance. It's a model district in every way. Why not try a district like Dhar?"

Ironically, that year the same model district played host to the brutal molestation and rape of nuns.

By the beginning of 1999, when the heat of the tragedy was on the wane (evident by the fact that the flood of national leaders to the district had been reduced to a trickle), the photographer Susan Bullough and I decided to travel to the district. The purpose of the visit was essentially to witness and photographically document the mood of a people caught in the national headlights like frozen deer.

Unsure of the prevailing law and order situation and the reaction a European would trigger off, I once again rang up the "relevant authorities" in Bhopal.

"What do you want to do in Jhabua? Anyway, you won't see much because the district is gearing up for Soniaji's visit. But you could, if you want, take a look at the place where those Christian missionaries got molested."

"No, that's not the purpose of this visit," I replied.

"If it's photos you want, the media already has a huge stock of pictures, you can use those," he persisted.

That was that.

So, Sonia Gandhi was headed to the place "where those Christian missionaries got molested." Good for her image.

We took a train from Delhi and late one evening got off at Meghnagar, Jhabua's only railway station.

Sonia Gandhi peered out at us from the peeling walls of the marketplace, from tea stalls, bus stand shelters, police chowkis...wherever there was space enough for her poster; she even fluttered from buntings and strings stretched across from roof to roof. She was everywhere. So were armed police and their bustling vehicles.

The prospect of hiring a jeep to take us across the district to Alirajpur was getting bleaker and bleaker until a Good Samaritan stepped in on the scene. And within an hour we were sipping our last tea in Meghnagar with the driver fidgeting at the wheel.

"Now it is dark," he said in Hindi tinged with a heavy dollop of *Malwi bhasha*. "Now it is dark," he repeated to himself. "We cannot go straight to Alirajpur. We have to first go across the border into Gujarat and then around from Dahod into Madhya Pradesh again...*seedha, phataak* into the district and then line to line, *seedha* to Alirajpur."

"What's the problem?" I asked. "Because of Sonia Gandhi?"

"No, not Soniaji problem. It is *goondaji* problem," he grinned. "The inside road is closed because there are Adivasi *dakus*. They come out at night. So we go the other way, from Gujarat side."

"There the road is not closed?" I asked.

"Yes but we have to go in convoy."

So we hit the road for Dahod and further still till we reached a convoy of trucks and cars. One long steamy smoky glowing snake, sliding along through the dark. Joining the tail end of the snake reminded me of the fate of tail-enders during Napoleon's retreat from Moscow. The Cossacks got them. Heh. But there weren't any Cossacks here but supposedly dangerous "Adivasi *dakus*." To be more precise — Bhil and Bhilala tribesmen who had, through the ages, been pushed against the wall. Stripped of their traditional hunting and food gathering lands, hunted down like vermin, and virtually forced into migratory labour, scattered, decimated, sometimes "tamed" in the plains regions into agriculturists practising alien religions — most often at the bottom of the caste pile.

The journey seemed endless. On the way vehicles peeled off and drove into byways until only our jeep remained. After endless bulleting into the dark, we were flagged down by armed guards and told to wait until other vehicles joined us to form another convoy.

The night pressed in around us, crowded with crickets and the ominous hum of the wind as it flowed through the deciduous jungle that stood along the sides of the road.

We had no intentions of sitting there in the middle of the night waiting for other vehicles so I climbed out and ambled over to the guard who sat perched on a creaky stool clutching an almost defunct bolt action rifle. "How long we wait?" I asked in my own brand of dialect.

"Long," he replied, spreading fingers of one hand outwards. "Long. Very long."

"Please let us go, we will go quickly. Fast, fast, we will be in Alirajpur. No one will know only."

"No fast fast," he replied, waving the fingers of the same hand. "No fast fast. You go, everyone will know. Also Adivasi arrow will know and find you easy. No going. *Bas*."

So I smiled and continued to hover around like an unwanted mosquito waiting for a quick sip.

If Strategy One hadn't worked, Strategy Two would. And what was Strategy Two? Chat up the unsuspecting victim.

"Many Adivasi *dakus* robbing lately, eh?" I asked.

He nodded.

"Very lately?" I persisted.

He nodded.

"Meaning just yesterday?" I went on.

"No, not yesterday," he replied, yawning.

"Then no problem," I said quickly, "we go."

"No," he insisted. "You think they're fools, eh? It is all a trick they play. One day they don't strike. Then everyone wait. Next day they don't strike. Everyone wait. And then third day they don't strike and everyone wait. So what everyone do? Start going and going only. Even late late night. Then *phut* one arrow comes and a scooterwallah will simply go zoom off the road with it sticking out of his neck. Or they will

'DO RATS HAVE RIGHTS?'

put big big stones on the road and a car will stop and the driver will go to move the stones and then the arrows come *chook, chook, chook* from everywhere...no, no, wait for convoy."

I had just about given up and turned to walk back to the jeep when he called out, "Okay, you can go now."

Those five magical words were more than just welcome. They were thrilling. The driver, who had stretched himself on a nearby concrete culvert, jumped up, pulled up his sagging trousers and stumbled towards the jeep.

He was just about to climb in behind the wheel when it happened...I sneezed.

The driver stopped almost in midair, got out and stared at me. The guard stood up, stifled another yawn and glared at me in disbelief. I had sneezed. That wasn't a good omen. "You can't go now," he said. "Bad luck. You sneezed."

So I returned to Strategy Two and started talking again, an exercise that all my friends, acquaintances and enemies will agree, comes quite easily to me.

Half an hour later, the man was so fed up with my babbling that he raised the wooden bar that blocked the road and signalled us to drive on.

Headlights cleaved through the dense darkness ahead and the road opened up before us like an endless muddy grey ribbon looping over undulating land. "No stones, no stones, no stones," the driver chanted softly to himself like he was reciting a mantra designed to ward off evil.

Then he suddenly slowed down and checked to make sure that the canvas flaps were well and truly secured. Even if they were, it would have been of no real help. An arrow from a Bhil or Bhilala short-bow could pierce through one side and sail out of the other if it missed...or slice an artery if it didn't.

Bulleting through the dark reminded me of the time in 1985 when I travelled at two in the morning from Alirajpur township to a place called Phata. My enthusiastic middle-level government official, tight as a tick, had decided to take the wheel. We were two kilometres down the road when one of his gunmen discovered that he had left his rifle magazine behind. Although the desperate guard kept calling out, the tick at the wheel continued to flash through the dark like Sterling Moss. "Bloody Bhil arrows, bloody Bhil arrows," he kept chanting.

Nothing seemed to have changed over the years. Only the manner of saying.

Anyway, the Malwa-accented driver continued to chant frenetically, "No stones, no stones, no stones," whilst the road looped away crazily like a ribbon in front of us.

"How long now?" I asked the driver.

He didn't seem to hear me because he was so ensnared in his mesmeric mantra.

I shut my eyes and when I opened them again we had hit the town of Alirajpur.

In the light of spluttering streetlamps Sonia Gandhi stared out at us from the dilapidated wall of a *paan* shop at the bus stand.

Nothing had changed. Only the face on the poster.

Would anything ever change in Jhabua?

I waited a year to find out.

'DO RATS HAVE RIGHTS?'

And so, late summer in 2000 A.D., we found ourselves with our Malwi-accented driver once again in Jhabua. This time, fortunately (or so I thought), we were travelling from the township of Alirajpur to the village of Jhinjhini.

It was like being suspended in time.

The sky was blank and pitiless, white light poured down on to the earth's cracked body, root-ribs protruding, worn smooth by the wind which carried the faint fragrance of *mahua* flowers and a flock of migrating swallows. Late summer flung dust-whirls, burning the edges of leaves, drying up pools of water, sending red-wattle lapwings into the air, spreading their haunting repetitions of an age-old question..."Did-you-do-it? Did-you-do-it?" Who had held back the rain clouds?

The flock of swallows appeared again, circled, swooped, settled on a derelict power cable, then disappeared into the low valley beside us that fell away into a jungle of stunted trees and shrubs.

The road (if one could call it that) from Alirajpur township to the village of Jhinjhini had begun with a "feel" of "progress" when we started off down its tarred surface but it soon became clear that illusion outweighed reality. Somewhere along its rambling passage, its skin of tar showed up tears and pits and gashes and wounds so deep that they could each conceal at least half a dozen bandits.

"The road's been that way for ages," a middle-level local administrator had earlier said, "that's why it was once considered to be one of the most dangerous stretches of road in the district of Jhabua ... I'd even venture to say, in the state of Madhya Pradesh, the country, in fact. Possibly in the whole of Asia...."
He flung his arms wide as he spoke, nearly knocking over the

167

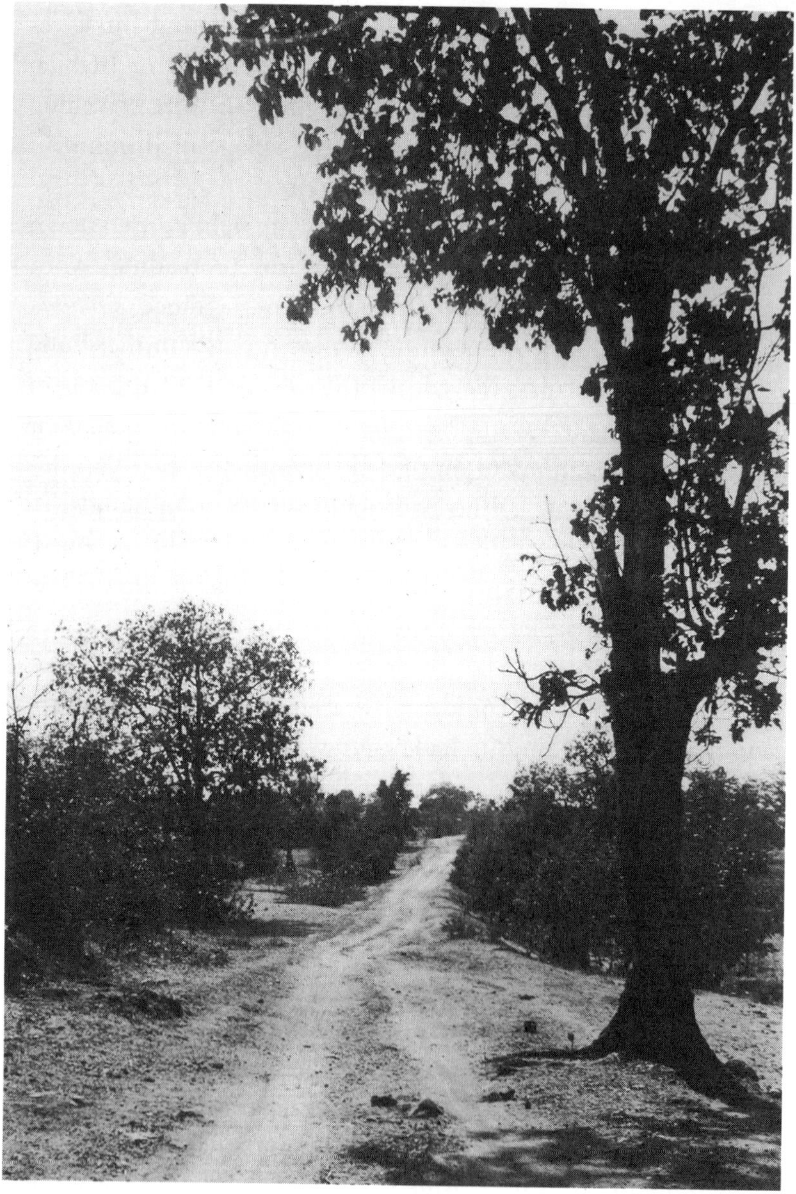

'DO RATS HAVE RIGHTS?'

glass of *taadi* which balanced precariously on a small roughly hewn table beside him. "But then, it's not the same now. Quite different. Peaceful. Crime? Pah!" he snorted.

"Yes," I wanted to comment, "so peaceful that the police station still resembles a fortress. High walls. Heavily barred gate. Or has it become a monastery?"

But I didn't. Instead, he picked up a piece of grilled jungle fowl, stuffed it into his mouth as if he was fuelling a muzzle-loader, and began talking again. Minute pieces of masticated fowl flew at me with each burst of words. So I stopped questioning him.

I'm sure that if I had continued listening to him, I would have been treated to a feast of more official overdoses about how the quality of life has only been changing for the better. According to most state government mouthpieces, the quality of life is always improving, particularly for marginal and minority communities. But the two words, "quality" and "better," are relative. Introducing publicity-mongering schemes doesn't really solve any problems because they are not really for the actual benefit of the people concerned.

The only reality was the haze of dust that was everywhere, shrouding half-naked trees with crinkled leaves and road-mouths lying hungrily open whilst swallows dive-bombed and rose again.

(Facing page) The road from Alirajpur township to the village of Jhinjhini showed up tears and pits and gashes and wounds so deep they could each conceal at least half a dozen bandits.

I could feel that we were being watched. It wasn't a comfortable feeling, I assure you. It was unsettling. But then I comforted myself that the sun was out.

"Even daytime also they do *loot-paat,*" muttered the driver, as if reading my thoughts. "Even daytime. They shot one fellow near that tree there," he said, pointing ahead down the road in front of us. And his scooter and body also went flying off into the *khud. Phoose,* it went, and the policewallahs found him later without any clothes on. Not even his *chuddies.* They are like that only. What will you do here?" he asked.

"Going to meet Bhoona Baba's family," I replied.

"But Bhoona Baba is not here only. He has gone off long back. To the other side. Meaning dead, *phataak,* gone," he said, "everyone dies only. Even he who is a powerful Badua.'

"Yes," I said quickly, remembering all the fellowship I had shared with that extraordinary human being. Locally referred to as a "Badua," Bhoona Baba was a shaman, storyteller, pithora painter and the unchallenged spiritual leader. "I know," I went on, "but I'm going to meet his family. I want to see how *they* are now."

He nodded knowingly and we drove on.

The jeep climbed a steep slope then descended down a narrow track through a newly-made forest of young teak trees. Far ahead, Bhoona Baba's homestead appeared, sunken amid cattle sheds, a couple of low-slung trees, axed woodpiles, handmade agricultural equipment, hay stacks and lantana shrubs.

> *(Facing page)* An Adivasi in Jhinjhini – *"Even daytime also they (Adivasi dakus) do* loot-paat.*"*

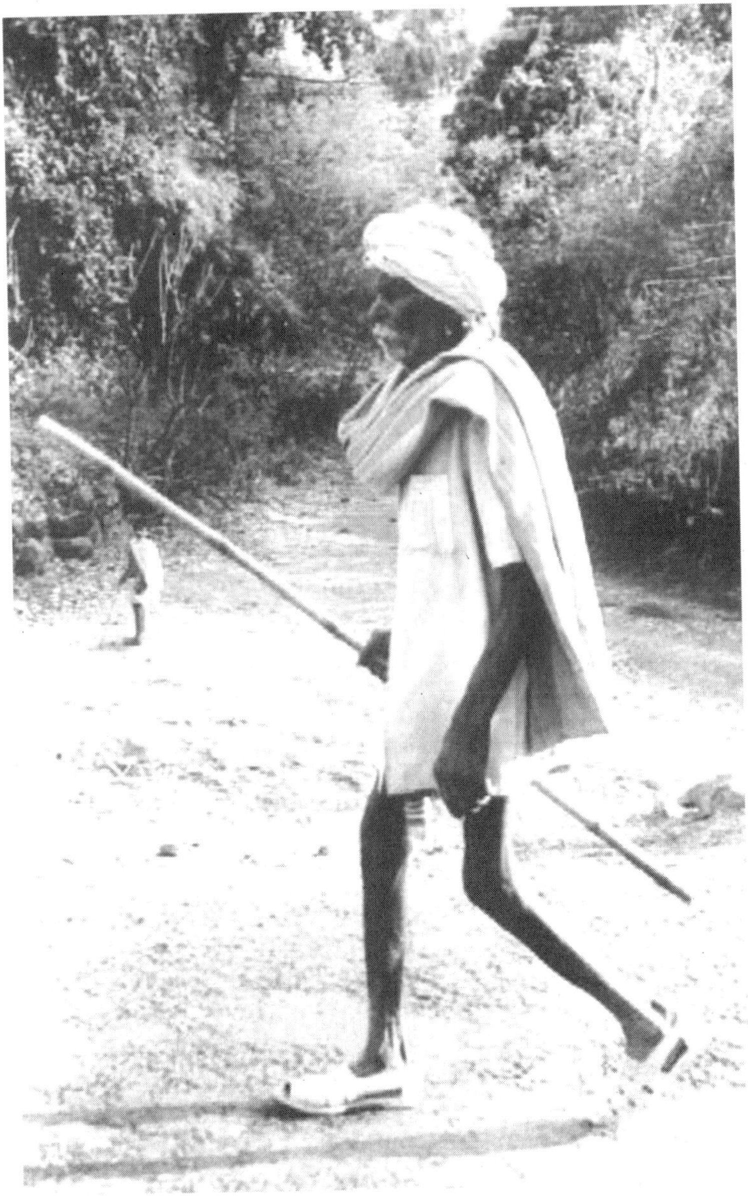

Innumerable thoughts and feelings flowed through me as we approached his home...the many times I had shared a drink with the man, exchanged stories, laughed, joked, trekked through the wilderness or just sat listening to him unravel legends of the Bhilalas and the Bhils as he sat hunched on the ground, drawing pictures in the dust...and then the last time I had met him. "The earth never changes, we change. I know that when I am gone, I will take with me all these memories, all that I have learnt, all that I have known and experienced in my life," he said, as we sat out the last night together, under the stars, on his *khatia*.

"No Baba," I put my hand on his shoulder. "Don't say that. It will go on as it always has gone on. It is destined...."

"Nothing is destined any more. I thought so once. Not any more. Nothing, my young brother. Nothing is destined. We now live in changed times. Destiny is a matter of the past. And *who* wants to know about the past?"

"But you have a family. Sons," I said.

"They have their lives. Viren is a teacher now. He has gone out into the world, leaving his old skin behind like a snake. And the younger one — he is simple. All he is concerned with is how to make the earth yield food and the cows and buffaloes offer milk. They are not interested in secret powers. They are not interested in all the hidden truths that I have gathered. It means nothing to them. They want things now. Things they can own. Things that everyone can see. Not hidden truths, hidden powers. Viren doesn't even want to talk about all this anymore."

There was about him a melancholic air as he rambled on, almost as if he had stumbled upon a terrible truth which made him feel that all that he had ever held as significant and meaningful was now suddenly redundant. The inexorable process of destruction was on and he sat there watching as all that he had held dear dissolved like the streams of home-fire smoke that curled up from thatched roofs and sailed through the spearheads of trees and scattered with the wind.

"Nothing will ever be like it used to be," he went on. "We live in strange times, brother."

"Yes," I said to myself softly, as we got out of the jeep and walked towards his home, "we live in strange times, brother."

Susan looked at me quizzically. "Said something?"

"Yes," I replied, pointing to the makeshift thatch roof which sheltered Bhoona Baba's memorial stone...."to him."

The Baba's distant relatives had appropriated most of his house and the surrounding compound. A tubby, well-groomed lady greeted us, then launched into a lengthy description of how she was related to Badua. I nodded and before I could collect my wits she had virtually pulled us into the verandah, sat us down on plastic chairs, all the while jabbering away about how she remembered me. I wasn't quite certain about who she was. I didn't remember having met her at any stage. Or maybe she had changed, grown plumper, changed her attire.

Out came sweet hot tea. Followed by a prolonged description of how the brickwork in the house had been extended. "This much we did already," she said, pointing to the pucca structure.

"Baba could have lived so comfortably if only he had agreed to do all this when he was alive," added the man who stood at the doorway staring at us indifferently, "and not lived in a *jhonpdi* instead. I cannot understand why he wanted to continue to live in a *jhonpdi*. He was such a stubborn man. He always said, 'We don't need more than this. This is enough.' His younger one accepted it and just went about tilling the plot of land, harvesting the crop, grazing the cows and buffaloes, milking them and that's about all. That's what he is doing at the moment. He is down by the lake, bathing the animals."

"What about Viren?" I asked.

"Ah ha. Viren," said the woman.

"Viren," echoed the man.

There was a respectful silence before they started talking. The woman made an early start. "He set out into the world, got married. He is a husband and a father."

"And a teacher," the man caught up quickly, almost puffing and panting to keep pace with his wife, swiftly lumbering past her. "He lives in the town of Umrali now. He is a wise fellow. He said that he didn't want to live in THIS sort of a village anymore. From Umrali he will go to the town of Alirajpur and from there to Indore and from there to Bhopal. Viren is a wise fellow. He looks at the future and does not care about the past."

"Who cares about the past?" asked the woman, half pointing out at Bhoona Baba's memorial stone. "That is why when we came from Indore to look after all this place, we told Viren that we will have to do it our way, not this Adivasi way... after all, this is the land of Ram Bhagwan."

The man nodded his head, widened his eyes and looked upwards at an invisible benefactor with spread-out hands.

"You want to meet Viren Master?" the man asked quickly. "It is very easy to find him. Just go to Umrali and ask for Viren Master. That's all."

Yes, I wanted to meet Viren Master. I wanted to talk to him and ask him whether he was happy doing what he was doing. Did he remember his father? Did he? Was he proud of his heritage? Ashamed of his past? Ashamed of where he had come from?

Whilst the two still continued to mutter about Viren's wisdom and the holiness of Ram Bhagwan's land, we walked away and rambled around the compound.

An eerie silence filled the afternoon air.

And then we left. Quickly.

Bhoona Baba's memorial stone stared out at us from under the thatch shelter near the boundary fence. Its brilliant blue face glowing in the shade. A mute reminder of the great and mysterious life of a Bhilala shaman.

We roamed around the village for a while. I, searching for faces that I recognised. Waiting for a smile. But what I got in return was a blank stare. Glazed eyes peering out of worn-out faces.

Families I had known hardly a year earlier had been scattered. Their young forced to go out and work in other people's fields, building other people's roads, playing in bands for other people's marriages, working as daily wagers in factories. Others, struggling with the land to make it bear fruit. The great machine was in motion. Approaching like a bulldozer to mow them down.

And so many had no option but to fight back.
Killing, looting....
Like they had done whenever they had been threatened in the past.

Popular opinion has always held that the Bhils and their relatives, the Bhilalas, are a savage, uncouth and "primitive lot." A mere glance at the various myths, legends and theories about their origins will prove revealing enough. For example, one legend says that they came into this world as the result of an incestuous union between a dhobi and his sister. There's also a Puranic account which claims that the first Nishada (ancestors of the Bhils) came from the thighs of Vena, the son of Anga who was childless. The first man was like "a charred log with a flat face who was extremely short." According to the *Bhagwata Purana*, he was "black like a crow and possessed a flat nose and blood-red eyes."

Here are a few more, plucked from the pile of "sacred literature." In the *Shiva Purana*, Lord Shiva was moping unhappily in a forest when a beautiful woman appeared to him. After a couple of rounds of seductive advances, she had sexual intercourse with him and cured him. The result of their roll in the bushes produced several offspring. One of them looked horrific and displayed foul manners. When he was old enough to challenge his father, he killed Shiva's favourite bull and got himself exiled to the forest. The first ancestor of the Bhil.

I'm tempted at this stage to take a detour and pussyfoot with you into the forbidden and controversial territory of the

'DO RATS HAVE RIGHTS?'

Eklavya story, or the account of how Parvati disguised herself as a Bhil woman and seduced Lord Shiva and broke his meditation on Mount Kailash, or the story of the Bhil who killed Lord Krishna with an arrow or about Valia the Bhil who became Valmiki who wrote the *Ramayana* (some claim it to be an invention of the Bhakti movement)...the deep-rooted implications of these accounts throw up a terribly sensitive area of debate which would overtake the overall objective of this essay. So for now, just for now, we will let them sleep, and wait for the right time when they can be awakened and all hell is let loose.

Colonel Tod in *Annals and Antiquities of Rajasthan* wrote, "The uncultivated mushrooms of India, fixed, as the rocks and trees of their mountain wilds, to the spot which gave them birth. This entire want of the organ of locomotion, and an unconquerable indolence of character which seems to possess no portion of that hardiness which can brave the dangers of migration, forbid all idea of their foreign origin and would rather incline us to the Monboddo theory that they are an improvement of the tribe with tails. I do not reckon that their raids from their jungle abodes in search of plunder supply any argument against the innate principle of locality. The Bhil returns to it as truly as does the needle to the north; nor could the idea enter his mind of seeking other regions for a domicile."

Almost without exception, hunter-gatherer communities have, down the ages, suffered at the hands of the herdsmen and cultivators who relentlessly axed or burned down trees and foliage, clearing forests. With the rise and growing presence of organised kingdoms, the pressure increased. Colonial occupation perpetuated the onslaught and the appropriation of forests by the state sealed their fate. Hunter-gatherers had become strangers in their own homelands.

The Bhil, traditionally a hunter-gatherer, was forced through time to scatter, across parts of Rajasthan, Gujarat, Madhya Pradesh and Maharashtra. Though the process of hybridisation has created varying social and cultural and economic patterns from community to community, the spirit of the Bhil has remained constant..."You have decimated my forest home, stripped me of all that was rightfully mine, driven my people like marauding cattle out of 'your' fields. And you continually suppress me and exploit me. I will hit back in the only way that is possible for me."

And so, what may appear to be a life of crime is in fact a life of revolt.

On 29 June 2000, *The Indian Express* carried a special report about the "the medieval custom" of the Bhils of six villages in the Mewar area of Rajasthan. Every *Chaturmaas* (from about the last week of June upto 11 July), just before the monsoons reach Rajasthan, they loot the houses and shops belonging to Jains in the area. The report says, "The tribals believe that the drought is brought by the prayers of the Jain community. 'They lock the monsoon clouds in their iron safes. Until we go and release them, the rains will never come,' says Nathu Bhil, a former village headman of Phalasia."

Interestingly, the report quotes Canda Bhil, a state government employee who also participates in the raids, as saying, "... the act of robbing is not for making money but for the ritual we perform. No one does it for the money we get from the safes of these Vaniyas (Jain traders)."

Later on in the report, the Udaipur collector chips in too, saying, "It is a tradition but it cannot be treated as a security threat." And a member of the Jain community comments, "It is a natural reaction to the fact that most of the village economy in the area has always been handled by Jains. So being slightly better off than the tribals, they were the natural target for expressing discontent." And the final blow is delivered by a resident of Udaipur, "What is really unfair is the fact that the attacks take place just a few days before the onset of the monsoon and the tribals' belief is reinforced that it is because they robbed the Jains that the rains have come."

A few days later, the paper carried a letter from a concerned reader in Pune who wrote, "After the promulgation of our Constitution providing several fundamental rights to all, the Bhil tribes are still allowed to remain ignorant of science and technology and are uneducated and follow age-old unscientific superstitions or *andhvishwas* because of which they still continue to rob the Jains." And he concludes his rambling argument with, "Even the laws provide for the customs of tribals to continue...certainly some of those customs which amount to crimes under the general law should not be allowed to continue at the cost of a particular section or community, in the democratic, secular Republic of India. The Bhils should be persuaded to drop this custom of robbing people of a particular community by proper education and their development should be given a special emphasis so that they become educated and start entering the jobs against the vacancies reserved for them in various local, state and Central services."

This reads like a cruel joke.

More than half a century of Independence has not made a difference. Imperialism is far from dead. It is alive and well in the Indian subcontinent. Both the report and the "concerned" citizen's point of view are soaked in it just like Christmas pudding is in a bottle of rum.

Neither the report nor the letter makes any effort to actually try and understand the predicament of the Bhil people. Both go on the assumption that since they — the letter writer and the reporter — belong to the faculty of literate, stable-living gentry, they are, therefore, entitled to voice their opinions as representatives of the Great Indian Mainstream. Further, their opinions are not based on any historical understanding or sensitive cultural reasoning but on a peculiar cocksureness which is the hallmark of superficial modernity.

How can we talk of the need for "development" and "change" among the Bhil people when we don't even have a notion of the Bhil identity, culture, traditional wisdom, religion and social practice? How can we understand the problems they face in their effort to stay alive and keep some semblance of self-esteem intact?

Innumerable studies have been conducted and books have been written on the Bhil people but unfortunately they are fit only for learned seminars, specialist libraries, doctoral studies and quasi-radical activists. The ones that escape the net are blighted by weak flaps of orientalism and do not present an accurate and realistic picture. Neither the print nor the electronic media has contributed much. If anything, they have often tended to sensationalise events rather than examine root causes.

So then, what is the general opinion and attitude based on? Assumptions.

Sadly, almost all tribal development planning at the district, block and village levels is also based on assumptions. Plans are devised and funds earmarked entirely on the basis of perceived needs of tribal peoples.

Very little effort is actually made to study a people and a region and to find out what their felt needs are. This has resulted in redundant programmes being set in motion, poorly supported by community contact and awareness programmes. The result — an enormous waste of resources, no trust or support from the communities concerned and an absolute collapse of local economies.

The Bhil people have been victims of this process. Instead of improving their lot, it has only perpetuated large-scale migration in search of employment, the rule of loan sharks and middlemen, unofficial bonded labour, prostitution... leading to reactionary crime.

Ironically, at the end of the day, the Bhil is the offender and we manage to save ourselves the guilt.

But I do believe that just because the Bhils are a marginalised people and fiercely outnumbered, their survival and growth should not be looked on as redundant. We live in a democratic republic and every community — however small — has the right to a life free from fear, oppression and exclusion.

And the solution?

Turn the tables.

Now is not the time to talk about bringing the Bhil people into the mainstream fold...now is the time to go out and try to record and understand them, historically, culturally, socially;

try to record and upgrade their traditional skills, try to provide a minimal support base for applying their traditional wisdom. The next step would be functional literacy, legal literacy, and economic and social literacy. This is a plea for restoration, for giving back to a displaced people a feeling of being wanted, a feeling of belonging. And the right to earn a living.

And from a practical and realistic standpoint, all this can be achieved by using the existing infrastructure and the existing financial outlays. But not in isolation. There has to be a sharing of government and NGO skills and experience. For far too long have we "used" tribal issues as cannon fodder. It is time for problem solving.

I suppose I have strayed far from that afternoon in Jhinjhini, so let me return to the sun slamming sparsely wooded hills with waves of heat and the fermenting smell of mahua burning its way into my lungs.

"Umrali," I said to the driver. "Umrali."

He stared out over the bonnet of the jeep at the broken road ahead, paused to say something then stopped himself and smiled. And then we were moving again, Bhoona Baba's homestead slipping out of view as we climbed the slope and bumbled ahead, the vehicle rocking as it edged around gaping ditches.

"Viren Master?" asked the driver. "Umrali. Viren Master?"

I nodded.

He nodded.

"He is not Adivasi now. He is something else. Different type person only. He is not like Bhoona Baba."

'DO RATS HAVE RIGHTS?'

I didn't respond.

We travelled in silence.

"You will also go to see Mission?" he asked, looking over his shoulder at Susan.

He didn't get a response. So he tried again.

"You will also go to see good work in Mission?"

I shook my head.

He finally gave up.

I remained doggedly silent for some time and then I began to wonder why I was being so non-communicative. I couldn't find an answer. The connecting cord had frayed and snapped. And there I was, suddenly a stranger. I looked at Susan and wondered what was going on in her head.

I began to feel suffocated and wanted to stop the vehicle, get out, climb on to the ridge running along the side of the road, spread my arms out wide, open my mouth and shout... nothing in particular, just shout...and free myself.

But of course, I didn't.

And we bumbled on. On past the police monastery with its massive walls....

Till the driver spoke again. "Now, we go fast fast," he grinned. "Good road."

It was early evening when we burst into the township of Umrali. We didn't have to spend any time searching for Viren Master's house. The driver took us straight there.

We descended purposefully from the vehicle and approached his place. A blast of bhajans poured out to greet us. Stopping dead in my tracks, I asked myself, "What on earth am I doing here?" Then I walked in to face the bhajans.

Viren appeared at the open door as we approached.

Although he recognised me, there was uncertainty written all over his face. What had I come for?

"What *seva* can I do for you?" he asked.

"Nothing," I said, "nothing. I was in Jhabua and thought I should drop in and see you."

"You went to Jhinjhini?" he asked.

"Yes."

He looked at me, waiting for some sort of an explanation. Elaboration. Anything. Anything that would assure him that I wasn't out to cause trouble.

I smiled reassuringly. "I went to see your father's memorial stone."

"And did you meet my brother?" he asked, anxiety already creeping into his voice.

"No. But your relatives were there...nice pucca work you're doing to the house," I quickly added.

"Not me. Them. They are doing pucca work. I am busy here. I have my work. There is school and other religious activities. You see, nowadays we have to do all that. Because that has got to do with our Indian culture."

His wife emerged with tea and biscuits.

The conversation went around in circles as I looked at the wall facing me. It was plastered with photographs. Viren Master with wife and children standing in front of the Qutab Minar. Viren Master with wife and children in front of the Taj Mahal. Viren Master with wife and children in front of an assortment of other monuments. Then Viren Master with a variety of dignitaries. Putting garlands, shaking hands, touching feet. Viren Master with his younger brother. Viren Master with other relatives. Marriage pictures of Viren Master. Even Viren

Master with his mother. But there wasn't any picture of Bhoona Baba, his father.

"Your father?" I asked but he pretended that he couldn't understand what I was trying to say. "Your father?" I asked again, my voice rising above the chants of the bhajans playing full blast.

I pointed at the wall. "Where is your father?"

"Dead," he replied and pointed upwards.

"I know," I continued, "but where is your father's picture? I don't see it there."

But he didn't seem to want to follow what I was saying.

"You want a photo of my father?" he asked.

"Yes," I said suddenly, trying to get him to face and respond to my question. "Is there one on the wall there?"

He looked at the wall full of photographs and then turned and said, "No photograph of my father there. No photograph."

"But everyone else is there," I commented.

"Yes, but he is not there. He is not there. But I have his photo. I have his photo. I am truly saying that I have his photo." His voice became noticeably anxious. Almost panicky. He searched among the books on two small shelves. "I have the photo, believe me," he kept repeating, almost to himself. Then he turned up the mattress of the small bed in front of us and pulled out folders and old magazines. Opened them, flipped through them. Then headed for the large Godrej cupboard. Opened it and started taking out clothes and books and other belongings, shaking them out, searching for his father's photograph.

When he had picked his cupboard clean, he put everything back, shut the doors and headed for the next room. Loud

185

mumbles and grumbles could be heard, counter-pointing the bhajans. It took a while for him to return. And when he did, he looked sheepish. "Not anywhere inside also. There is one I gave to a studio. And I told them to make a big photo. In that there is my father and brother and myself. We are looking very modern there. Even my father looked nice nice. Not *junglee* type. Meaning he was dressed very nice."

The term, "not *junglee* type," immediately opened up an image of Bhoona Baba. Short, lean, grey tousled hair, a red headband, necklaces of coloured beads spread across his bare chest...crouched on the side of the road outside his house, patting the ground near him. "Sit sit," he had said, looking up at me, "sit here and listen to the wind coming. Can you hear it? We will soon have rain."

"But there aren't many clouds," I said, looking up at the sky.

"The wind is speaking. Listen. Listen. There is a message of rain."

And by nightfall, cloud banks piled up and it rained steadily all through the night and the hills were whipped and their great boulder-sides whined and moaned in the dark which was sliced by lightning.

"He was dressed very nice," Viren Master repeated. "Meaning white shirt and dhoti. Very nice."

It was evident that the man was ashamed of his father because the shaman represented his own tribal past, his roots, his identity...all that he was desperately trying to reject, all that he was trying to dissociate himself from, bury, forget. Sure, he had got his school master's position on a "tribal ticket," but once he had got it, a whole new world of possibilities opened up to him. A new, stable and acceptable religion and all the trappings of "mainstream living"...provided that he "integrated" and forfeited his tribal identity.

"Very nice. Very nice...." His voice trailed off and he looked at me, embarrassed.

We exchanged a few pleasantries, dissolving the tension in the room. Then left.

A couple of days later we took a bus out from Alirajpur to Indore, the white sky promising no rain, the air heavy with fermenting mahua.

The last summer of the century. The last summer of the millennium.

II

The rains came. Finally. Wave after wave. Carried by the southwesterlies. Up along the coast, trailing silver sheets from Kerala onwards to the Konkan. The Arabian Sea heaving and rocking in the wind.

The rains came. Finally. Turning inwards from the coast, colliding with the Western Ghats, then climbing up and over. Greening the dry craggy hillslopes. Grass, weeds, reeds, bushes, trees, moss...green, green, fluorescent green. Wild flowers flashing orange, yellow, blue, sparkles of red.

Time for hunter-gatherers to harvest edible wild roots and shoots from the shrinking jungles.

Time for promises of survival.

I sat in the makeshift teashop near Malavali railway station (close to Lonavala in the state of Maharashtra), tucked into the foothills of the Western Ghats, a steady thump of rain-fists beating on the battered tin roof above me.

The *chaiwallah* placed a glass of steaming tea on the wooden table in front of me. "*Vada pau?*" he asked. I nodded.

I had just about taken the first bite of *vada pau* and followed it quickly with a deep sip of *elaichi* tea when a swarm of flies descended from the ceiling. The tabletop soon became a runway. Batches of flies would take off, hover, harass, get swatted at, swerve and land...giving another lot the opportunity to go in for the attack.

The amazing display of aerial combat entertained me whilst I munched on my well-guarded morning snack. "More tea?" shouted the *chaiwallah*. I nodded.

When he placed the glass in front of me, he said, "Make sure you don't put any food on the bench next to you. There's a hole in the gunny sack just behind and it'll get picked up."

"What'll get picked up?" I asked.

"The food," he said.

"How?"

"A dog or a cat or a mongoose or a Katkari will take it. *Zook*, and it's gone. Just like that. Just two days ago, a customer was sitting right here where you are sitting and he ordered a plate of four *vada paus* and he put it on the bench. He got busy talking with me and then when he put his hand down to pick up a *vada pau*, there was nothing there. Gone. All four. Just then I looked up towards the road in front here and saw some Katkaris coming up from the side of the shop and climbing on to the road. One of them was eating a *vada pau*. So we went

'DO RATS HAVE RIGHTS?'

out and caught them. The one who was eating a *vada pau* handed back the half-eaten piece. The others had the *paus* in their mouths and we couldn't get them back. This is what they keep doing. They never come in here and order tea or buy *vada paus*...." His voice trailed off.

"Because they don't have money," muttered one of the customers, an old sadhu on his way to the mandir near the caves at Karla. Running the palm of his right hand gently over the lawn of silver hair on his perfectly spherical pate, he sighed as if the weight of the world was resting on his shoulders.

"They don't have money because they spend it all on drink," added another customer, stuffing the hole in his face with a *khari* biscuit soggy with tea.

"They should just live in the jungle where they always have. They were born *junglees* and will remain *junglees*," said the *chaiwallah* finally.

"But it's not their jungle any more," I said.

"Who says so?" asked the *khari* biscuit-slurping one.

"The forest department," I replied.

"But there's no jungle here anyway," said the one with a silver lawn on his head, "it's all gone. *Junglees* are *junglees*. They cut down all the trees. Killed all the animals and ate them up. And now that they have no jungle left they are coming out here to steal and feed."

The others nodded in agreement.

Just then, a ragged group of men and women walked past in the rain. Pieces of jute sacking, plastic sheeting and torn cloth draped around them. "There they go," said the *chaiwallah*, looking at me, "Katkari field labour. I know these ones. They are Dalvi's labour. His fields are on the other side of the track but they are wandering about in this direction. And it's work time already." Then he yelled out to them, "Hoi, hoi, what you doing here? Dalvi Seth will beat you with a stick...go, go back."

They turned around and laughed, then continued walking in the rain. One of them shouted, imitating the *chaiwallah*, "hoi, hoi." And the others joined in.

"See," said the *chaiwallah*, "that is their level."

"A jackal will be a jackal," said the one with a silver lawn on his head, "you cannot expect it to be a tiger."

I paid the bill and walked out into the rain. Paused for a moment, looked down the road at the ragged group retreating and headed after them.

One of them stopped and looked over his shoulder, saw me waving, then nudged the others to stop.

When I reached them, I stood there wondering what to say. I smiled. They smiled.

Then I did an odd thing. I walked past them. Slowly. Kept walking. Turned and smiled again.

"So where are you off to?" asked a wizened old one among them, speaking in a broken combination of Marathi and pidgin Hindi.

"Walking," I replied.

"To the mandir?" asked a younger one.

"No. Just walking."

We walked in silence.

"And where are you going?" I asked.

"Just walking," said the wizened one.

"Off to get Ramu," said the younger one.

"No, Shyamu," said another.

And they all began to play around with rhyming words. Everything that even vaguely rhymed with the original word, "Ramu."

"So Ramu is your child?" I asked.

They all started laughing loudly. "It is a *bakri, bae, bae, bae*," said the wizened one. The others imitated him. So I added a "*bae*" for good measure.

It turned out that they were off to pick up a small goat from a settlement nearby. To be slaughtered and eaten, of course. Two of them went off the road, slipped between a hedge and returned a while later, "Ramu" in tow. A coal black creature with large frightened eyes and a string of marigolds around its neck.

Having collected Ramu, the group trudged back down the road.

I trailed along with them. "That *bakri*, you robbed?" I asked.

"No, no, no," they all shouted and laughed. "On loan. Take now, kill now, eat now, pay little little...after."

When we passed the teashop the *chaiwallah* called out, "Hoi, do you know who he is? He is a *patrakar*. He will put your life story in the paper and then everyone will know about you."

"You are a *patrakar*?" the wizened one asked me.

"No. I write. Books," I replied.

"And what do you do with the books you write? Keep them in a big box?" he persisted.

"People read them."

"So if you write about us, people will read our story?" he went on.

I nodded.

"*Hut saala*," he said jovially to himself. Then he asked, "you give these books free or people pay money for them?"

"People pay money for them," I replied.

"*Hut saala*," everyone said in unison.

Then the wizened one went on, "Imagine, people pay to read our story. Everyone does business with our lives and we go on like this, *hut saala*...." And they all laughed.

We walked on in silence for a while. One of the younger men hoisted Ramu on to his shoulders.

The railway tracks had already been crossed and we ambled down along a slushy road, crossed a newly constructed expressway and headed on.

The rain had mercifully let up a bit and only a steady drizzle sprinkled around us. Not far ahead, on the other side of the expressway, the land climbed slowly up into a craggy hill, densely wooded in some patches and velvety green with grass and weeds and shrubs in others. Higher up, clouds sailed by, colliding with the rockfaces, stopping, merging, dissolving and growing again. Curls of smoke from unseen huts pushed their way up from among the trees, lazily floating along till they got themselves absorbed by the gauzy clouds above.

The wizened one slowed down till he was walking beside me. The rest of the group laughed and chatted as they strolled ahead, in no particular hurry to get to Dalvi Seth's fields... that is, if they were meant to go there as the *chaiwallah* had suggested. "Kishen," the old man said, jabbing his chest with his right forefinger. "Kishen."

I introduced myself in the same manner.

He shook his head knowingly, grinned. "Mumbaiwallah?"

"Punewallah."

"Hmmmm. Mumbai is a *jaadu* city. I know. They took many islands and stuck them together with cement and stones and all. Now so many people living there that it has become very heavy and all the cement and stones are breaking and soon all the islands will be separate. You cannot do *masti* with nature. See here, we do not do *masti* with nature. See up there where the smoke is going up from? That's where Katkaris live. And every house is on a slope so rain water drains off. Nothing gets blocked. Nothing, I tell you. See, everything is clean here."

"And your house," I asked, "where is your house?"

"There in that field there," he pointed.

Sure enough, out in front of us was an open field which was divided into small paddy seedling nurseries. On a few slightly raised areas in the middle were low slung thatched huts.

"That your land?" I asked.

Kishen laughed and slapped me on the back. Then laughed again. I joined him, slapping him on the back. "My land? Hah haa! My land, my land, my land, that is my land," he kept repeating.

The group walking in front of us jovially joined him, "My land, my land, that is my land," they repeated over and over again.

"Then how you stay there?" I asked.

193

"The Seth says I can stay. I do this and that for him because I stay there," he replied.

We walked on.

Kishen didn't look like he had a care in the world. To hunter-gatherers, the moment is of primary importance. They are tuned to the moment, to life around them, the time of day, to the season, the signs of nature, to the language of the wilds. And it is because they are so tuned that their senses are heightened. They are acutely aware of even the most subtle throb of life near them or around them. And it is this acute awareness of their environment that has helped them realise their position in the web of life...not as masters but as participants. This realisation and acceptance has always been the common foundation shared by all hunter-gatherer communities in the country, including the Kurumbas, Irulas, Saheriyas, the more secluded communities of Bhils and Bhilalas, the Andaman Islanders and a myriad small groups struggling to keep alive in various parts of the subcontinent. The common attitude and approach to their natural environment has always been — "Take only what you need to survive this moment. Nothing more."

This attitude and lifestyle has always been seen by "the others" as shortsighted and primitive. "The Katkaris of this region," Nandkumar Padmule, the sarpanch of Bhaje, a village near the Katkari settlements, had told me a few days earlier, "are like buffaloes. They can only see the grass that is in front of them. Nothing else. They think for the moment. If that is

*Kishen, the Katkari tribal — without a care
in the world, and tuned to the moment.*

not laziness and stupidity, what is?"

"But what are they to do?" I asked him. "They are traditionally hunter-gatherers and perhaps also marginal farmers. That's all. How can you expect them to be anything else?"

"What hunter-gatherers are you talking about?" he asked. "There are no forests left. No animals. No birds. Nothing. And what are they going to gather? Some wild fruit and some *jari-booti* and all. What else? Firewood. That's all they do... go out every day and collect firewood. And then sell it in the village. What else? If the times have changed, then they have to change. They can't possibly be a burden on our village. First they lived in the forest, now they are living near the village. They scraped around to survive in the forest, now they do the same thing here. Our country is going forwards, not backwards. So they have to change too. I give them five years more and they'll all get wiped out."

"Padmule Sahib," I said, gritting my teeth, then relaxing my jaws into a soft smile, trying to avoid unnecessary confrontation, "they were here long before your village even existed...they lived in the forest that once was here. They had a very special relationship with the forest because it was their home. Would you take off the doors of your house and use them for firewood, Padmule Sahib? You certainly wouldn't. Similarly they weren't going to destroy their own home."

"Then how did these hills become bare?" he asked, almost like a challenge.

"When non-forest people came here," I tried to put it simply.

"You mean us?"

"Yes," I said. "When all the villages sprang up. Where do you think the firewood came from all these years? Don't you think it's unfair to blame the Katkaris for this?" I asked, pointing to the empty hills.

"I don't think so, because I'm right," he replied. "How do you think I became sarpanch?"

I couldn't understand the man's argument. So I stayed quiet for a while, sipping tea from an enormous glass.

He got up and left, swaggering on to the open dust track, barking commands at a group of workmen.

I watched him as he walked up the track and vanished around the corner. Then I began to think about what he had said. Sure, it was evident that he had become sarpanch because he had the support of the village heavyweights. They were the ones who had the money, social position, caste backing. He'd never be in that position if he had started supporting the cause of the Katkaris. They had nothing to offer him. No money, no social position, no caste backing. Nothing at all. Why should he back losing horses?

In a society where marginalised communities have nothing to "give" the ruling class, the likelihood of any type of support coming their way will always be bleak. This has been the lot of the Katkaris. Their entire way of life has always excluded, to a great extent, other communities. Their world has always been the forest and they've lived according to the laws of the forest, moving from place to place and region to region as hunter-gatherers...taking from the forest only what they needed, replenishing on the way. Their survival inextricably linked to the survival of the forest. And in this natural rhythm of taking and giving, land ownership never appeared a necessity. The Katkaris have never believed that land can be "owned." Land, they believe, is the gift of life, to be savoured and preserved for generations to come and not raped and pillaged. It is divine and cannot be owned.

However inspiring this may seem, the very fact that they have never been a settled people and never believed in ownership of land, has left them at a distinct disadvantage. Boundaries of state and private territories have grown everywhere. Free movement without violating "someone else's" space is hardly possible anymore. Their forest abodes have been destroyed and they have been forced to live on the fringes of other community settlements like scavengers, eking a living by daily wage earning on marginal agriculture plots and construction sites and on trucks as cleaners.

The Katkaris have never been as interactive and socially responsive as the Bhils and as such have always avoided confrontations. Although at some stage in the distant past they may have shared similar hunter-gatherer lifestyles, the Bhils were uprooted and forced to scatter — living by their wits in a rapidly changing historical, political and social scenario. The two aren't the same anymore, and yet they share a common fate — decimation.

If the life of the Katkaris is so miserable and isolated and there doesn't seem to be any hope whatsoever, why am I babbling on about their "cause" like a soapbox orator?

I believe that the fate of the Katkaris is linked symbiotically with the fate of our forests. To survive — they need each other. And we must be able to see this need clearly and honestly and respond to it positively.

I do not suggest here that ownership of forests be handed over to communities like the Katkaris. That would be a stupid and shortsighted thing to do. But I do suggest that they be made an integral part of all reforestation and forest protection and maintenance programmes. They have the traditional wisdom and skills for such work and they will be able to contribute more than adequately.

And my suggestions for their inclusion don't stop here. Taken further, they should be included in horticulture programmes. The idea would be to apply their forest-based traditional wisdom and skills to contemporary forest and horticulture programmes and in the process upgrade these skills.

But then, in order to set programmes like this in motion, it would be necessary for an integrated approach to "tribal and forest management." A number of state governments have attempted the same approach but have got themselves tied into a tangle of red tape because all development programmes in our country have happened vertically — the left hand unaware of what the right hand is doing. Integrated action demands an integrated vision, a holistic approach.

Realistically speaking, even if such a holistic approach was to be adopted, the first step to be taken would be (as I had suggested in the first part of this essay) to try to understand the Katkari identity, socially, culturally, economically, religiously, ecologically. This would lead us to an understanding and awareness of the traditional wisdom and skills of these hunter-gatherers. It is only when we have understood this that we can plan and work towards integrated programmes. Planning without understanding amounts to working on the basis of assumptions.

Coming back to that enormous glass of tea and Sarpanch Padmule's divine utterances and his subsequent departure....

I got up to leave.

The Sarpanch returned. "Did I tell you, sir," he beamed, striding back jauntily, "that I'm planning to computerise the whole village?"

"And what about your neighbours, the Katkaris?"

"What about them?" he asked.

"What about their rights?" I persisted.

"Do rats have rights? Do they? Tell me sir, do rats have rights?"

"Are you saying that they have to be exterminated? Is that your solution?" I wanted to know.

"Oh, no one has to do it for them. They'll do it themselves. They drink, they eat all sorts of meats. They don't plan for the future. Because they are illiterate, they do not even know their rights and how to make use of the development funding that is available for them," Nandkumar bumbled on.

"So you're the sarpanch here, what are you doing about it?"

"Me? Oh, I tried so hard. I even went and caught one family and got them a loan from the bank for fishing activities and got their children into school. But then what happened? They are all collecting firewood once more. An ungrateful and ignorant lot." He pulled up his legs and crossed them, then waving his hands as if delivering a speech, he said, "There are so few of them here that it doesn't make a difference if they are here or not."

"But," I persisted, "do you see a solution?"

"A solution? Yes — money power. If they have money power, they have a future. What else can I suggest?"

Nandkumar's adamant refusal to even try to understand the predicament of Katkaris, isn't unusual. Similar attitudes and responses exist wherever hunter-gatherer and marginal farming tribal communities come in contact with "the others" who are "socially, technologically and economically more organised." In fact, I would like to even stretch it further to towns and cities where so-called progressive minded people consider matters related to "tribal survival and development" irrelevant and totally out of sync with the "times"...and communities like the Katkaris, primitive, wretched and bound for extinction.

A comment by John Wilson about the Katkaris, which was published in the *Journal of the Royal Asiatic Society of Great Britain and Ireland* in 1843, proves the point that after all this time and more than fifty years of independence, attitudes have not changed.

"They are the most degraded body of natives with whom I am acquainted...they live, as outcasts, near villages inhabited by other classes of the community. They are held in great abhorrence by the common agriculturists, and particularly by the Brahmans; and their residences are wretched beyond belief. Their miserable units are situated where all the refuse of the village is thrown, and they have companionship with all that is impure. Looking to the position in which they are found...we can scarcely fail to associate them with the words of the Revelation — 'without are dogs and sorcerers.' "

For now, I'll let the argument lie and return to my companions and myself (along with a goat named Ramu), walking along one rainy morning in the foothills of the Western Ghats.

Kishen was still on the subject of huts. "We build our homes ourselves," he said, "with wood and twigs from the jungle. You come, I will show you. No windows. No rain can get in. No sun can get in. No wild animal can get in. Nothing can get in. When we go away in the jungle or go away to some distant field to work, we just leave all this here. On the way, we build another one. All we need is two trees. One *danda* from one tree to another and another *danda* and another and some branches and leaves and twigs and *bas*, we are ready."

"What happens when you don't find two trees?" I asked.

"Then all we need is a big rock and we put some branches and leaves on the side and...*bas*," he said confidently, "we have a home."

"What about food when you travel through the jungle since there are no more animals and birds?"

"Who says so?" he asked angrily. "But then we don't only kill and eat animals and birds. There are plants there that we can eat and roots...," he stopped in mid-sentence, then waved his hand regally at the wooded hill and the others beyond clothed in clouds, "that is our market, our kitchen, our home. Everything. For you it may seem as if there is nothing left but for us it is still our bank."

The pride with which he spoke reminded me of that famous line from Rajpipla Bhil lore — referring to the Satpura mountain range which is the home of their High God: "To you it is stones and hills, to us it is heaven."

"Ah, ah, we have reached. Home," he said, holding me by the arm.

Just then a tall and well-built "other," wielding a six-foot bamboo lathi, came around the bend, shouting, "Where have you all been? You were to come to the Seth's fields this morning. What are you roaming around here for? You will come at once, you hear me? You hear me?"

The gang walking in front of us scattered.

"Come back, will you? Come back at once," the man shouted, banging his lathi on the road, "what will I tell the Seth?" Then he turned to Kishen who stood cowering near me, "You are an elder, can't you beat some sense into their heads? But then you are no better. You come along now. Sir, please explain to him. Just because he has enough money just now, it doesn't mean that he should not do any work. Please explain." He stopped for a moment and looked at me quizzically. "Who are you, Sir?" he asked. "Social worker?"

I shook my head.

"Professor?"

I shook my head again.

"You do not look like a Party type so you must be a *patrakar*."

"Writer. *Lekhak*."

"Why are you wasting your time with these people? Can you make any money writing about such people? But that is your business...," he looked around frantically. Kishen had evaporated, vanished, while we were talking. "See, they are very smart at slipping off. What to tell them." He headed off towards the first hut.

He stood outside the hut and rapped on the low thatched roof with his lathi. "Oh, come on out, come on out, come on out. You hear me? Come on out...."

I walked up to him and said, "Why don't you go in."

"Go in?" he asked, almost choking. "Go in? You just have to stand here to get the smell. This place stinks. It stinks. Don't go near that door," he warned.

"Where's the door?" I asked.

"Down there," he pointed.

I moved closer and saw a small square doorway a few feet off the ground. One would have to crouch to pass through it — going in or coming out. "Kishen!" I called out but there was no reply. So I went even closer and bent down to peer in. Then the smell hit me, square in the face. I don't know how to describe it. At first it seemed like the stench of something rotten, like meat or dead rats. And I recoiled. I paused, then bent down again. "Kishen!" I called out. A muffled voice responded and it sounded somewhat like, "Come on in."

As I got accustomed to the stench, it didn't seem like that of dead rats but an overpowering smell of moist, musty earth that had not seen daylight or felt fresh breeze ever since the hut was built. Added to that was the smell of perspiration and uncured goatskin.

"Don't put your head inside," warned the man with the lathi, "you'll get sick."

"Kishen," I said softly, ignoring the warnings of the "other", "Can I come in?"

"Yes," he said.

So I crawled in, ignoring the stench.

My eyes slowly got accustomed to the dim light thrown by an oil lamp which stood in one corner and I was surprised to find that the hut was jampacked with people. Somehow, everyone had decided to heave their way in. There was a giggle, a grunt, the goat started bleating, a baby cried. The "other" stood outside rapping the thatched roof with his lathi and calling out to them.

Then we heard him leave.

After a while, Kishen said, "Now he is gone, we will go out."

I was the first to make it through the small square hatch. Followed by others.

Outside, I stood there gasping for fresh air, afraid that I was going to puke and offend everyone present. But thankfully, I didn't. I held my composure, washed my face and was myself again. "You are living on the Seth's land, how can you not do his work for him?" I asked Kishen.

"This is another Seth and that is another Seth," he said.

And everyone laughed.

In a small clearing, near Kishen's hut, two children played with the goat, feeding it leaves and stroking its back. The small flimsy garland of marigolds around its neck had snapped and there was a trail of petals from the doorway to where it stood.

"You saw my house?" asked Kishen. "You like my house?"

I nodded.

"You want to go to jungle houses on the hill?" he raised his eyebrows. "You want to?" And before I could answer he called out to one of the younger men, "*Hoi* Anand *re*, you are going to Babu's house, eh? You are going, eh?"

"Yes, now."

"Take him with you."

And so we set off.

Anand broke into a trot across the electric green field towards the base of the craggy wooded hill. I stumbled along behind him, trying furiously to keep pace. "*Chalo, chalo,*" he shouted, without looking back. "*Chalo, chalo.*"

Then he reached the first big boulder and scaled up along its side, reached its shoulder and hopped along from boulder to boulder like a mountain goat. I followed, trying the same hop, step and jump but went sliding all over the place. Sanity prevailed and I quietly followed the well-used path that went weaving off between the shrubs...upwards. Somewhere from high above came Anand's voice, "*Chalo, chalo.*"

When I finally reached the first shoulder of the wooded hill, two huts emerged from the foliage. They were silent. No sign of anyone. Further up the slope towards the next shoulder, other huts were partially visible. Smoke rose from them. But I still couldn't see any people.

I couldn't see myself climbing up all that way, over slippery rocks and an almost vertical jungle path streaming with slush. "*Chalo, chalo,*" Anand called again.

The rain saved me. I heard it coming a few minutes before it arrived. It was like a giant rock exploding after being hit by a thunderbolt. The first blast of water hit the side of the hill horizontally. Trees and shrubs were momentarily flattened and then sprang back again in slow motion as the velocity of the wind decreased and the rain slipped into a

'DO RATS HAVE RIGHTS?'

steady downpour. Then the next blast came, the rainy wind striking a nearby hill, bouncing off its side and glancing sideways, horizontally along the hill on which I stood, like a knife across a victim's throat.

"*Chalo, chalo,*" I could still hear Anand's cry, "*Chalo, chalo.*" Blown away by the wind, across the rain-swept Western Ghats...till only the cry and squeak of whipped branches could be heard. The wind finally broke through a tree barrier and knocked down one of the huts nearby. It tilted, fell over and disintegrated, sections quickly scattering through the foliage...reeds and leaves and thatch leaping into the air like streamers. Fortunately, it was an abandoned hut and no one was hurt.

I crawled into the other hut that was left standing. Some time later, Anand joined me. He jabbered away about the storm and the wind and how I wouldn't have been stuck there if only I had exercised some courage and gone up the slippery vertical hillside. I swallowed my pride and sat quietly.

Evidently, no one was in the hut. Anand said that the man of the house had died in the jungle some time back and the woman had taken her children and gone to stay with some relatives. She would return, perhaps with another man, leaving her children with a relative.

Whilst I sat there in silence, the man talked on, letting loose a stream of information about their marriage, birth and death rituals, hunting, fishing, eating habits, bows, arrows...the words came thick and fast. He was, in his own way, taking me through a Katkari package tour. At first I wanted to silence him — the rain and wind and the rooty dark inside of the hut with its primordial assault on my olfactory organs had been so unsettling that I was becoming disoriented; his fuselage only added to the turbulence. But then I realised that he was so used to those sorts of conditions in the wilds that it hadn't occurred to him that I was undergoing some sort of trauma.

And the more this realisation grew on me, the more I became aware of the fact that I was privileged. There was I, a "nobody" in their community, accepted in without suspicion. They needn't have made the effort. Kishen needn't have shared so much of his life with me. Anand needn't have taken me all the way up the side of the hill.

Most importantly, their acceptance of me had nothing to do with the hope of receiving bakshish of any kind. It was merely an expression of a natural respect for and acceptance of another living being.

It became increasingly obvious that they were spontaneously expressing and demonstrating very strong community values and community etiquette...all of which had been nurtured and developed down the ages. Although to many of the "others" they were uncouth, unhygienic, animal-like, uncivilised, unreliable, it was evident that they were more humane, just, uninterfering, unprejudiced and nurturing than all their neighbours put together. They were themselves and didn't pretend to be anyone else. Living close to nature, they had learnt the value of sharing. They had learnt to be inclusive and not exclusive.

Sitting there in the damp darkness of the abandoned Katkari hut in the Western Ghats, I listened to the rain beat mercilessly down on the thatch and the leaves of the trees and grass all along the hill slope, and the rocks too, and on the hills nearby harbouring Katkari families...and the other hills of the ghats all the way down the coast along the Konkan region...and across to Thane and Raigad.

This was their home. This is their home. Their land. Their forest. Their birthright.

Sitting there, with the fetid odour enveloping me, I felt suddenly humbled.

When the rain lessened to a drip, we walked out. "You are going to Pune?" he asked.

I nodded.

"Go down that way. He pointed to a path that went down between the trees along the other side of the hill. "It will reach down in front of the highway. Then you walk across and there is the railway station."

Before I could thank him he was gone. He had slipped away silently.

I stood there, alone, breathing in the wet air, heavy with the aroma of broken green leaves and branches. Then I picked up the path and wandered down.

Half-way, I decided to change direction and instead turned left down another track and headed off along the side of the hill towards the village of Bhaje where it sloped off and rose again, touching the shoulder of another craggy hill which housed the prayer caves of first century B.C. Buddhist monks.

The hills all around were alive with waterfalls, some streaming and dripping, others bouncing along...and still others straight-dropping hundreds of feet, exploding on large slabs of glistening rocks below and streaming with foamy mouths

First century B.C. Buddhist caves — two thousand years and more ago, the Buddhists had come to the forest kingdoms of the Katkaris to find peace.

downwards to the fast-flowing rivulets in the valley below.

The jungle was alive with an amazing variety of butterflies, some flashing blues and reds and yellows...others with deeper hues of purple and black. A painted spurfowl dodged across the path and white breasted kingfishers echoed their shrill, haunting cries along with the wind that had settled to a soft moan.

I sat for a while on the roughly hewn floor of the Buddhist prayer hall. Wet clothes clinging to my skin. Gradually, very gradually, the turbulence inside me settled like silt in river water. I knew of course that it would not be long before the tide came in again and swirled the silt to rise...but for then, for those few moments, I knew I could be still, would be still.

Two thousand years and more ago, the Buddhists had come here to seek solitude in the wilderness, to carve prayer caves from nature's rocky flesh...to meditate on nature's myriad metaphors. Two thousand years and more ago, they had come, to celebrate the universal spirit of nonviolence. Two thousand years and more ago, they had come, to reflect on nature's lessons of unity in diversity, of the equality of all forms of life — however big or small...irrespective of colour, appearance, feeding habits, growth patterns and seasonal variations. Two thousand years and more ago, they had come to the forest kingdoms of the Katkaris, to find peace, salvation.

Notes on Contributors

MEENAL BAGHEL is currently an associate editor with *The Indian Express* in New Delhi. Previously she has worked with *Mid-Day* in Mumbai, and with *Pioneer* and *The Asian Age*.

SIDDHARTHA DEB grew up in Shillong in the North-east, moving to Kolkata to study English Literature. He has worked as a journalist with national publications in Kolkata and Delhi. Since 1998, he has lived in New York City, where he is a Marjorie Hope Nicholson Fellow at Columbia University and is working towards a Ph.D. in English Literature. His first novel will be published by Picador in 2002.

SAGARIKA GHOSE is a Delhi-based writer. She was educated at St Stephen's College, Delhi University and at Oxford University where she was a Rhodes Scholar. She began her journalistic career with the BBC World Service in London before moving on to *The Times of India* in Delhi. In 1995, she joined *Outlook* magazine, where she wrote on social issues and politics. She is the author of the critically acclaimed novel, *The Gin Drinkers*.

MUZAMIL JALEEL is currently the Kashmir bureau chief of *The Indian Express*. Based in Srinagar, he has been reporting on Kashmir affairs for nearly a decade. He was awarded a fellowship by the *The Times of India* group in 1994 to work on, "Implications of violence on Kashmir society."

AJIT KUMAR JHA studied politics in New Delhi, Oxford and California. He was the resident editor of *The Times of*

NOTES ON CONTRIBUTORS

India, Patna and is now a senior associate editor of *The Indian Express* in Delhi.

RANDHIR KHARE is an award-winning poet and writer who has published nine volumes of poetry, fiction, travel and a novel-length fable. His experiences among the Bhils, spanning nearly two decades, have culminated in his translation of their song-poems into English, collected in a volume entitled *The Singing Bow*.

SANKARSHAN THAKUR is the author of *The Making of Laloo Yadav — The Unmaking of Bihar*. A Delhi-based journalist, Thakur has also written for the other two books in the Contemporary Essay series: *Guns and Yellow Roses — Essays on the Kargil War*, and *On the Abyss — Pakistan After the Coup*.

VIJAY JUNG THAPA has been a journalist with *India Today* and *The Times of India*. He is currently an editor with explocity.com, a city-centric website.